[business minds]

FINANCIAL TIMES
Prentice Hall

In an increasingly competitive world, we believe it's
quality of thinking that will give you the edge – an idea that
opens new doors, a technique that solves a problem,
or an insight that simply makes sense of it all. The more you
know, the smarter and faster you can go.

That's why we work with the best minds in business and
finance to bring cutting-edge thinking and best learning
practice to a global market.

Under a range of leading imprints, including *Financial Times
Prentice Hall*, we create world-class print publications and
electronic products bringing our readers knowledge, skills
and understanding which can be applied whether studying
or at work.

To find out more about our business publications, or tell us
about the books you'd like to find, you can visit us at
www.business-minds.com

For other Pearson Education publications, visit
www.pearsoned-ema.com

Pearson
Education

[business minds]

connect with the world's greatest management thinkers

Tom Brown, Stuart Crainer, Des Dearlove &

Jorge Nascimento Rodrigues

FINANCIAL TIMES
Prentice Hall

an imprint of Pearson Education

London • New York • San Francisco • Toronto • Sydney • Tokyo • Singapore
Hong Kong • Cape Town • Madrid • Paris • Milan • Munich • Amsterdam

PEARSON EDUCATION LIMITED

Head Office:
Edinburgh Gate
Harlow CM20 2JE
Tel: +44 (0)1279 623623
Fax: +44 (0)1279 431059

London Office:
128 Long Acre
London WC2E 9AN
Tel: +44 (0)20 7447 2000
Fax: +44 (0)20 7240 5771
Website: www.business-minds.com

First published in Great Britain in 2002

© Pearson Education Limited 2002

The right of Tom Brown, Stuart Crainer, Des Dearlove and Jorge Nascimento Rodrigues to be
identified as Authors of this Work has been asserted by them in accordance with the
Copyright, Designs and Patents Act 1988.

ISBN 0 273 65660 0

British Library Cataloguing in Publication Data
A CIP catalogue record for this book can be obtained from the British Library

All rights reserved; no part of this publication may be reproduced, stored in a retrieval system,
or transmitted in any form or by any means, electronic, mechanical, photocopying, recording,
or otherwise without either the prior written permission of the Publishers or a licence
permitting restricted copying in the United Kingdom issued by the Copyright Licensing
Agency Ltd, 90 Tottenham Court Road, London W1P 0LP. This book may not be lent, resold,
hired out or otherwise disposed of by way of trade in any form of binding or cover other than
that in which it is published, without the prior consent of the Publishers.

10 9 8 7 6 5 4 3 2 1

Designed by Claire Brodmann Book Designs, Lichfield, Staffs.
Typeset by Northern Phototypesetting Co Ltd, Bolton
Printed and bound in Great Britain by Biddles Ltd, Guildford & King's Lynn

The Publishers' policy is to use paper manufactured from sustainable forests.

[about the authors]

Tom Brown is CEO and Publisher of Brown Herron, a company that sells e-docs exclusively on Amazon.com. He is also the creator of the Management General website (*www.mgeneral.com*). The author of popular e-books such as *The Anatomy of Fire: Sparking a New Spirit of Enterprise* and *Fiscal Fairy Tales,* Tom has contributed to publications worldwide including the *Wall Street Journal*, *Across the Board*, and Harvard's *Management Update* newsletters.

Stuart Crainer and Des Dearlove are the founders of Suntop Media (www.suntopmedia.org), the world's leading thought-leadership content provider, as well as the creators of the Thinkers 50, the first ranking of business gurus (*see* www.thinkers50.com). They are the authors of *Firestarters!, Gravy Training, Generation Entrepreneur, The Financial Times Handbook of Management*, and *MBA Planet.*

Jorge Nascimento Rodrigues is editor of *www.janelanaweb.com*, a management and technology trends portal, and writes for *Expresso*, a weekly newspaper published in Lisbon, Portugal. He is the creator of www.gurusonline.com.

"Creative thinking is today's most prized, profit-producing possession for any individual, corporation, or country. It has the capacity to change you, your business, and the world."

Robert P. Crawford

[contents]

contents

contents

The intellectual war among the business gurus is ongoing. To stay at the top requires boundless reserves of mental and physical stamina. The gurus travel the world unceasingly. Seminar follows seminar. If it's Tuesday it is probably a 45-minute speech to the Baltimore Brewing Federation; Wednesday could be Minneapolis or Madrid; Thursday, Toronto or Tokyo.

And the guru circuit is becoming more crowded. The leading players are so well rewarded that their example encourages emulators. Every year a battery of books and articles proclaim the rise of new management gurus. Recent years, for example, have seen the rise of the new economy thinkers. These digital gurus now vie with established old economy thinkers to map out the business landscape of the future.

All of this makes it increasingly difficult for practicing managers to identify and stay abreast of the latest and best business thinking. Idea after idea is launched with ever louder fanfare. And the trumpeting gets more strident. A fountain of new books gushes from publishers and new and established authors.

Why ideas matter

To some people, of course, the merry-go-round of new (and not so new) ideas and thinkers is no more than a side show to the serious business of business. Yet the simple fact is that modern management is a curious mix of the practical and the theoretical. Ask a manager which dominates and he or she will naturally say the former: management is about getting tasks done. Yet the reality is more complicated. None of us can afford to entirely ignore new ideas.

A growing number of managers have now been to one of the many business schools around the world. For these people, schooled in management theory, the power of ideas is understood. But those who did their management training in the school of hard knocks may ask: "Why bother?" They might argue, with some justification, that management is fundamentally a hands-on activity and has little relation to the grandiose or ethereal theories of management gurus.

It is easy to dismiss much of what is written and disseminated through conferences and seminars as irrelevant to what real managers do on a day-to-day basis. It is easy to assume that they continue to do what they have always done. But the fact is that new ideas and concepts shape how we think about the role of managers in a changing business environment.

Think about how the job of the manager has changed in the past few decades. What is needed in today's business world, it is almost universally agreed, is a lighter touch on the reins, a more intelligent use of human resources, and a more empowering style of management. Today the manager is seen as a leader and facilitator rather than controller and policeman. At the same time, the sort of environment and organization in which managers operate is changing to fit new conceptions of what a business should look like. The fundamental understanding or psychological contract between the manager and the organization is being transformed by redefinitions of the employee/employer relationship.

Where do such notions come from? From the management thinkers, of course. From the thousands of business books, articles, case studies, and models that are produced each year. These have a constant drip, drip, drip effect on the consciousness of managers everywhere. A steady flow of new ideas is redefining what managers should be doing, how they should be doing it, and, critically, how their job performance is evaluated. Today's theory is often tomorrow's task.

Just as the best theory is (or should be) derived from the real world, so the real world is changed by the promulgation of the theory. The great business school and consulting concepts are theory created out of prac-

jectivity is vital. What distinguishes their ideas from the flavor of the month flotsam? We've tried to select thinkers who have delivered, or have the potential to deliver, significant and lasting benefits – or a lasting impact in other ways. Most have some of the following characteristics:

- timeliness – the issues they address meet an immediate need or anticipate one that is not yet recognized;
- self-containment – even though they are built on earlier ideas, the best thinkers stand on their own. They can be understood in isolation from what came before;
- real-world credibility – either from extensive research or experience at the sharp end of business, and preferably both;
- intellectual rigor – the quality of thought and insight is another distinguishing feature of true thought-leaders. Some ideas are deliberately vague to allow universal application. Great ideas are razor sharp; they have their own internal logic. They are consistent and provide useful definitions;
- simplicity – the best ideas are derived from basic, universal principles. They are intuitive. They help us make sense of the world around us;
- practicality – perhaps the real difference between fads and ideas that last is their usefulness to managers – their practical application.

Happily, the Thinkers 50, the global guru index, confirms that many of our selections would also have been chosen by practicing managers.

The Thinkers 50

First published in January 2001, the Thinkers 50 (*www.thinkers50.com*) ranks the most influential living business thinkers. Developed by Suntop Media, it provides the only authoritative global ranking of business gurus.

Thinkers 50 2001

	NAME
1	Peter DRUCKER
2	Charles HANDY
3	Michael PORTER
4	Gary HAMEL
5	Tom PETERS
6	Jack WELCH
7	Henry MINTZBERG
8	C.K. PRAHALAD
9	Bill GATES
10	Philip KOTLER
11	Peter SENGE
12	Sumantra GHOSHAL
13	Warren BENNIS
14	Rosabeth Moss KANTER
15	Robert KAPLAN & David NORTON
16	Nicholas NEGROPONTE
17	Kjell NORDSTROM & Jonas RIDDERSTRÅLE
18	Stephen COVEY
19	Percy BARNEVIK
20	Jerry PORRAS & James COLLINS
21	Ed SCHEIN
22	Kenichi OHMAE
23	James CHAMPY & Michael HAMMER
24	Andy GROVE
25	Michael DELL
26	Chris ARGYRIS
27	H. Igor ANSOFF
28	Alan GREENSPAN
29	Richard BRANSON
30	Jeff BEZOS

[warren bennis]

leadership optimist

a business mind with a passion for leadership

In 1996, *Forbes* magazine referred to Warren Bennis (born 1925) as the "dean of leadership gurus." Indeed, while there are many authors and speakers with books and rousing presentations on how to become a leader, Bennis has written and spoken more on leadership, advised more corporate and government leaders (including four US presidents), and has himself served in more leadership roles than any of them.

With a distinguished academic career with roles ranging from president of the University of Cincinnati to chair of organizational studies at MIT's Sloan School to professorships at Harvard, Boston University, and the University of Southern California, he also has served on the boards of the American Chamber of Commerce, the Claremont University Center, and the Salk Institute.

Bennis is the author of 26 books, appearing in more than 20 languages. His classic, *Leaders* (1985, Harper & Row), was named as one of the 50 best business books of all time by the *Financial Times*. His most recent book with David Heenan is *Co-Leaders: The Power of Great Partnerships* (1999, John Wiley), which focusses on those "number two" people who work quietly behind the scenes in support of many well-known leaders.

In May 2001, The Marshall School of Business at the University of Southern California, which Bennis currently calls home (*www.marshall.esc.edu/more/*

people/BennisW.html), hosted a "festschrift" – a celebration of his 40-year career with a conference devoted to his scholarly work which included luminaries such as Peter Drucker, Charles Handy, Tom Peters, as well as top business leaders, educators, and journalists.

In this interview, Bennis demonstrates his mastery of leadership by projecting the traits of a leader in *tomorrow's* society.

Do you see yourself as a romantic?

If a romantic is someone who believes in possibilities and who is optimistic then that is probably an accurate description of me. I think that every person has to make a genuine contribution in life, and the institution of work is one of the main vehicles to achieving this. I'm more and more convinced that individual leaders can create a human community that will, in the long run, lead to the best organizations.

Do great groups require great leaders?

Greatness starts with superb people. Great groups don't exist without great leaders, but they give the lie to the persistent notion that successful institutions are the lengthened shadow of a great woman or man. It's not clear that life was ever so simple that individuals, acting alone, solved most significant problems. None of us is as smart as all of us.

So, the John Wayne type of hero is of the past?

Yes, the Lone Ranger is dead. Instead of the individual problem solver we have a new model for creative achievement. People like Steve Jobs or Walt Disney headed groups and found their own greatness in them. The new leader is a pragmatic dreamer, a person with an original but attainable vision. Ironically, the leader is able to realize his or her dream only if the others are free to do exceptional work. Typically, the leader is the one who recruits the others, by making the vision so palpable and seductive that they see it, too, and eagerly sign up.

Inevitably, the leader has to invent a leadership style that suits the group. The standard models, especially command and control, simply don't work. The heads of groups have to act decisively, but never arbitrarily. They have to make decisions without limiting the perceived autonomy of the other participants. Devising and maintaining an atmosphere in which others can put a dent in the universe is the leader's creative act.

But isn't this somewhat unrealistic?

True. Most organizations are dull, and working life is mundane. There is no getting away from that. So, these groups could be an inspiration. A great group is more than a collection of first-rate minds. It's a miracle. I have unwarranted optimism. By looking at the possibilities we can all improve.

What will it take for future leaders to be effective?

The post-bureaucratic organization requires a new kind of alliance between leaders and the led. Today's organizations are evolving into federations, networks, clusters, cross-functional teams, temporary systems, ad hoc task forces, lattices, modules, matrices – almost anything but pyramids with their obsolete top-down leadership. The new leader will encourage healthy dissent and values those followers courageous enough to say no.

This does not mark the end of leadership – but rather the need for a new, far more subtle and indirect form of influence for leaders to be effective. The new reality is that intellectual capital (brain power, know-

how, and human imagination) has supplanted capital as the critical success factor; and leaders will have to learn an entirely new set of skills that are not understood, not taught in our business schools, and, for all of those reasons, rarely practiced. Four competencies will determine the success of new leadership.

What's first?

The new leader understands and practices the power of appreciation. They are connoisseurs of talent, more curators than creators. The leaders are rarely the best or the brightest in the new organizations. The new leader has a smell for talent, an imaginative Rolodex, is unafraid of hiring people better than they are. In my research into great groups I found that in most cases the leader was rarely the cleverest or the sharpest. Peter Schneider, president of Disney's colossally successful Feature Animation studio, leads a group of 1200 animators. He can't draw to save

The new reality is that intellectual capital (brain power, know-how, and human imagination) has supplanted capital as the critical success factor

his life. Bob Taylor, former head of the Palo Alto Research Center, where the first commercial PC was invented, wasn't a computer scientist. Max DePree, former CEO of Herman Miller and author of *Leadership is an Art* (1989, Doubleday), put it best when he said that good leaders "abandon their ego to the talents of others."

Then, second, the new leader keeps reminding people of what's important. Organizations drift into entropy and the bureaucratization of imagination when they forget what's important. Simple to say, but that one sentence is one of the few pieces of advice I suggest to leaders: remind your people of what's important. A powerful enough vision can transform what would otherwise be routine and drudgery into collectively focussed energy. Witness the Manhattan Project. The US Army had recruited talented engineers from all over the United States for special duty on the project. They were assigned to work on the primitive computers of the period (1943–5), doing energy calculations and other tedious jobs.

But the Army, obsessed with security, refused to tell them anything specific about the project. They didn't know that they were building a weapon that could end the war or even what their calculations meant. They were simply expected to do the work, which they did slowly and not very well. Richard Feynman, who supervised the technicians, prevailed on his superiors to tell the recruits what they were doing and why. Permission was granted to lift the veil of secrecy, and Robert Oppenheimer gave them a special lecture on the nature of the project and their own contribution.

"Complete transformation," Feynman recalled. "They began to invent ways of doing it better. They improved the scheme. They worked at night. They didn't need supervising in the night; they didn't need anything. They understood everything; they invented several of the programs we used." Feynman calculated that the work was done "nearly ten times as fast" after it had meaning.

brain

Charles Handy has it right in his book *The Hungry Spirit* (1998, Broadway Books). We are all hungry spirits craving purpose and meaning at work, to contribute something beyond ourselves, and leaders must never forget to remind people of what's important.

Trust is a small word with powerful connotations and is a hugely complex factor

power

What else does a new leader strive for?

The new leader generates and sustains trust. We're all aware that the terms of the new social contract of work have changed. No one can depend on life-long loyalty or commitment to any organization. Since 1985, 25 percent of the American workforce has been laid off at least once. At a time when the new social contract makes the ties between organizations and their knowledge workers tenuous, trust becomes the emotional glue that can bond people to an organization.

Trust is a small word with powerful connotations and is a hugely complex factor. The ingredients are a combination of competencies, constancy, caring, fairness, candor, and authenticity – most of all, the latter. And that is achieved by the new leaders when they can balance successfully the tripod of forces working on and in most of us: ambition, competence, and integrity.

And, lastly?

The new leader and the led are intimate allies. The power of Steven Spielberg's *Schindler's List* lies in the transformation of Schindler from a sleazy, down-at-the-heels, small-time con man who moves to Poland in order to harness cheap Jewish labor to make munitions which he can

then sell to the Germans at low cost. His transformation comes over a period of time in which Schindler interacts with his Jewish workers, most of all the accountant, Levin, but there are also frequent and achingly painful moments where he confronts the evil of the war, of the holocaust. In the penultimate scene, when the war is over and the Nazis have evacuated the factory, but before the American troops arrive, the prisoners give him a ring, made for him, from the precious metals used by the workers. As he tries to put the ring on, he begins crying, "Why, why are you doing this? With this metal, we could have saved three, maybe four, maybe five more Jews." And he drives off in tears.

It is hard to be objective about this scene; but, though this was a unique event, it portrays what new leadership is all about: that great leaders are made by great groups and by organizations that create the social architecture of respect and dignity. These new leaders will not have the loudest voice but the most attentive ear. Instead of pyramids, these post-bureaucratic organizations will be structures built of energy and ideas, led by people who find their joy in the task at hand, while embracing each other – and not worrying about leaving monuments behind.

If you go into a company, what's the most important question you ask?

On a scale from 1 to 10, 10 meaning 100 percent and 1 meaning close to zero, how much of your talent is being deployed in your job? And why?

What question would you like to ask the managers of the world?

How do you learn?

[james champy]

change engineer

a business mind who grasps the fundamentals of real change

James Champy (born 1942) is chairman of the Perot Systems consulting practice. Formerly, he was chairman of CSC's consulting group and co-founder of CSC Index. He is also a member of the MIT Corporation, the board of trustees for Massachusetts Institute of Technology.

A leading authority on management issues surrounding business reengineering, organizational change, and corporate renewal, he is the co-author (with Michael Hammer) of the now classic *Reengineering the Corporation* (1993, HarperBusiness), which was on the *New York Times* bestseller list for two years. His follow-up book, *Reengineering Management* (1995, HarperBusiness), was named by *BusinessWeek* as one of the top management books of 1995 and was named by Peter Drucker as "the definitive book on the subject."

His newest book, *The Arc of Ambition* (2001, Perseus), was written with Harvard professor Nitin Nohria. While many would find the subject a surprising one, Champy says he had strong reasons for following reengineering with a book on ambition: "When people stop and think about it, they recognize that some form of ambition drives them – that what we often talk about as 'leadership' is actually the residue of ambition. I believe managers would all be better leaders if they understood the source and nature of their ambition."

Champy moderates programs for the PBS Business Channel and writes columns for *Forbes*, *ComputerWorld*, and *Sales & Marketing Management* magazines. More information about Champy can be found on *http://www.perotsystems.com/frm-baseasp?URL=/content/AboutUs/Leadership/james.asp*.

In this interview, he outlines what makes a reengineering effort successful and where the reengineering movement is making the most difference.

Reengineering is often seen as ambition gone haywire, especially by the general public.

That is because the reengineer's motivations are too often simply assumed. As change agents, we don't have to talk openly about our ambition, but we should examine it carefully. We should look at the quality of our ambition – for what purpose do we strive? Is there a "greater" purpose in what we do beyond just generating profits? Too often we experience the ambition of others as overreaching and failure. Most people talk and write about ambition in that way. Sometimes well-intended people get to a point where they believe themselves infallible – like a Bill Clinton – and they do foolish things. That's what we see. We don't see the really good ambitions of Bob Shapiro, the former CEO of Monsanto, who wanted to figure out how to feed the world.

Has the reengineering movement been positive?

I think that the balance is very positive. In global terms, I think that we have only reached 10 or 20 percent of what we intended, so there is still a lot to be done. At this moment there is a very real reaction to reengineering that comes from people who do not understand the concept. Many consider it very similar to the downsizing trend. Others have not yet understood the need for a fundamental change in the way in which

corporations work. Reengineering is exactly that – it is a radical change in the way people perform their work in corporations. The basic idea of reengineering is now a global phenomenon. More than a management fad and a buzzword, it is really a genuine need.

Which sectors of the economy had the best results?

I am not sure that there is a clear answer to your question. I can name those industries that, in my opinion, should urgently start reengineering projects. In the first place are the industries linked with technologies, the telecommunications, and media enterprises. Your business (press), for example, is a strong candidate for reengineering because your industries are making a revolution in the history of information and of publications. In the second place are the financial services, the banks in particular, whose reengineering isn't done yet. Then there are the health services. In the US, maybe more than in Europe, the health system is suffering vital changes. Then there are the public utilities which live in a phase of deregulation and privatization around the world. Last are the transport industries, which stand to reap great benefits from reengineering that presently are being lost.

Were there reengineering differences between Europe, the United States, and Asia?

In cultural terms, I think that North American managers are better prepared to be radical and to cut with the past. In Europe generally, managers are more conservative. Some countries, such as France, are heavily influenced by socialist traditions. But in Germany, there is recognition of the necessity of applying reengineering. Germany is one of the better markets nowadays to apply the concept. Although the Germans are conservative, they are very much aware of the need for change, particularly in the automobile sector. In Asia, I have seen reengineering in locations like South Korea, Japan, and Hong Kong. Of these, the Japanese are the ones who show more willingness to try to do things differently.

Why the Japanese?

The Japanese are facing a great challenge because they are not moving as fast as their competitors in the management of change. That is one of the motivations for Japanese corporations to build new plants outside of Japan. Change is easier to implement because the culture is less resistant. With the Koreans the situation is different. They are more open to foreign ideas and ways of thinking. The Chinese, on the other side, still do not have reengineering infrastructures in place, because their businesses are like collections of small operations. In spite of everything, they seem to be facing the change well.

How will the dramatic changes you talk about manage to take place?

Without being ironic, I think that each corporation needs a shrink. My work is to persuade the manager to see the market in a different way, to understand the level of change that is adequate, and to agree about the necessity of making changes in how work is done. That is without any doubt the most difficult part. I think that the techniques related to process redesign are easy to understand and implement. Those linked with great cultural changes are more complicated. That is due to the fact that the managers still have, in my opinion, a traditional way of thinking. The change I talk about is radical and discontinuous, not incremental, contrary to what we are used to daily.

Are consultants *required* to implement reengineering?

Companies will probably learn to do it by themselves, but, in my opinion, not with the greatest change efforts. Companies still do not know how to change strategy, the processes, the technology, and the culture simultaneously, without external help. It will still take ten years until the muscle of management will be capable of doing it. The reengineering movement still has to go through all the steps that strategy has already passed. Ten years ago, the best consultant companies that specialized in strategy were growing at a good pace – McKinsey, Boston Consulting Group, Bain and Monitor, Michael Porter. On a large scale that business decreased due to the fact that managers learned to develop that discipline. Nowadays people know that the way to a good performance doesn't lie only in having a brilliant idea or strategy, but also in looking at the processes. I think that the consulting firms still have about five to ten good years of reengineering work. After that, it is probable that there will be a new phase of accommodation.

Nowadays people know that the way to a good performance doesn't lie only in having a brilliant idea or strategy, but also in looking at the processes

How long is a reengineering journey?

In my opinion, the complete journey takes two to three years. But there should exist concrete results in the first 12 or 18 months, otherwise the resistance to reengineering will certainly grow.

And to counter that resistance?

Many people don't understand the subtleties of managing. They believe that a manager must be decisive, that the world is black and white. In fact, a good bit of the business world today is gray; you may not know immediately what to do. It's okay to think for a while. There is a lot of intellectual work to management – but that counters the macho approach that managers often adopt to maintain power. Operating only through control diminishes your power to lead people. It suggests that you really don't know what's going on.

When you go into a company, what is the most important question you ask?

I always like to ask an executive what he or she is "going through" to get a sense of what they are experiencing and what his or her agenda is. It's an important starting point to trying to be of help and give legitimate advice.

What question would you like to ask the managers of the world?

I would like to ask the managers of the world what their aspiration is for their business. It tells me something about what they value and what they are most likely to accomplish.

[peter cohan]

e-master

a business mind with a keen sense of why e-success happens

While many are fretting over how to use the Internet, Peter Cohan (born 1957) has been relentlessly striving to understand the root causes of Internet success and failure. He has kept a detailed log of his learnings by writing a series of bestselling books: *The Technology Leaders* (1997, Jossey-Bass), *Net Profit* (1997, Jossey-Bass), and *e-Profit* (2000, Amacom). His fourth book focusses on *e-Stocks* (2001, HarperBusiness).

Cohan has an above-average interest in how the markets mesh with the e-world. He is a commentator for the CNBC cable channel, and his stock analyses have routinely yielded a high rate of return. Validea.com calculates a 52 percent six-month return on his 2000 stock picks. Bigtipper.com recognized Cohan as the top tipper of 1998 for the 68 percent return of his CNBC stock picks. His 1999 stock picks returned 239 percent. TeamAsia called Cohan "one of the top two or three technology strategists in the world." Singapore's Institute of Advertising called him "the Peter Drucker of the new millennium."

"As an investment analyst," Cohan says, "I am known as someone who has developed a useful perspective on how to value technology investment opportunities by synthesizing industry and competitive analysis, organizational change management, and traditional financial analysis to create a framework for picking under- and over-valued securities."

His ability to sense what may be happening next on the Internet has made him a quotable authority. He is often cited in publications as diverse as *Business 2.0, BusinessWeek, Barron's, CBS MarketWatch, Fortune, Le Monde, The Times* of London, and *USA Today*.

Having worked at CSC/Index with James A. Champy and at The Monitor Company, co-founded by Professor Michael E. Porter, Cohan now operates his own company. More about him can be found at *www.members.theglobe.com/petercohan.*

E-business is now almost universal, with lots of knowledge about how to conduct business online. Are we *there* yet? Do we have state-of-the-art e-business?

With all the hype, one would believe that all businesses are taking full advantage of the Internet. The reality as I have seen it is that no more than 5 percent of the companies out there are taking advantage of the transformative power of the Internet. For example, the US Commerce Department estimated that the value of retail e-commerce in 2000 was about $25 billion, which represents less than 1 percent of US retail sales. Despite this, interest in e-business remains high.

And one could argue that the demise of the dot.coms is a healthy development. Between 1995 and 2000, too many executives found themselves scrambling to do something to avoid being Amazoned. This fear led executives to spend billions on Web consultants and infrastructure to develop e-business strategies to defend against a threat that began evaporating when the Nasdaq plunge began in April 2000. The dot.coms made companies aware of the potential benefits of e-business, and their collapse makes it possible for traditional companies to exploit these benefits in a more deliberate fashion. The firms that rise to the challenge of using the Internet effectively will be able to create and sustain competitively superior value for their customers, employees, shareholders, and suppliers.

So, what *is* e-business?

Many people have been led to define e-business somewhat narrowly as selling consumer products online. My definition of "e-business" is the use of the Internet as a tool to create superior value for a firm's stakeholders – specifically the firms' customers, employees, shareholders, and suppliers. The implications of this definition are profound. Rather than focussing on ways that the Internet can be used as a way of selling more, managers should start by thinking of how they create value for each of their stakeholders relative to competitors. For example, managers need to think about questions such as:

● What criteria do customers use to choose between our firm and competitors?

● How do the best employees decide whether to join and stay with our firm versus their peers?

● What business environment attracts and keeps the best suppliers working with our firm instead of our competitors?

● What characteristics draw the most loyal investors to our firm and keep those investors from parking funds with our competitors?

In answering these questions, there is an opportunity for a firm to change its strategy, organization, and business processes to tilt the playing field in favor of the firm. And in making these changes, the Internet can facilitate the changes and sustain competitively superior value for these stakeholders.

Will e-business doom traditional businesses?

The winners will be those who can blend best-of-breed virtual capabilities with best-of-breed physical ones. For example, a merger between Amazon.com's Web site and Wal-Mart's ability to cut great deals with suppliers and fill each store with the most in-demand items at each location would create an unbeatable cluster of capabilities. The winners will be those that can seamlessly integrate an organization with world-class virtual and physical capabilities to deliver an unbeatable customer value proposition.

What about e-management?

E-management, to me, means the ability to implement what I've been talking about in a way that generates consistently outstanding financial results. E-management shares four features of traditional management while presenting a set of four unique challenges. The shared characteristics are:

- the performance imperative: the need to generate consistently outstanding financial performance (as measured by earnings growth, return on equity, and stock price performance) is just as strong in the traditional world as in the e-world;

- attracting and motivating top people: an enduring reality of management is that the winning firms are the ones that can attract the best people and motivate them to do the right things;

- what's measured gets done: an important way to attract and motivate the best people is to create an effective performance measurement system that makes it clear to people how their activities are linked to outstanding financial performance. While this concept sounds simple, its effective execution makes the difference between a well-managed company and its peers.

● breeding the next generation of management is Job 1: While some e-companies were built to flip, the long-term leaders recognize that creating the next generation of leadership is the most important responsibility of the CEO. Many may end up emulating Jack Welch, who used a combination of astute hiring, job rotations, mentoring, and training to breed a very deep subs' bench at GE.

And the unique challenges?

I'd cite these:

● *Need for mastery of the virtual and physical worlds:* the best e-managers recognize that customers will give more of their business to companies that offer more value for less money. Winning e-managers know that delivering a superior-value proposition means sustaining world-class capabilities in both the virtual and physical worlds.

Winning e-managers know that delivering a superior-value proposition means sustaining world-class capabilities in both the virtual and physical worlds

Simply put, e-management demands a sort of managerial ambidexterity which is as rare as it is valuable.

- *Skill at positioning the firm within a network of industries:* e-management also demands the ability to see how the firm fits into a broader system of value creation. E-management is different because doing it well requires the e-engineering of broad business ecosystems. Such systemic e-engineering demands the ability to enhance the value in not just a few business relationships but an entire system of such relationships.

- *Ability to filter signal from noise:* e-management demands the ability to be connected to thousands of inputs about specific changes among many industry participants such as suppliers, customers, employees, competitors, media, and shareholders. Effective e-management requires the ability to monitor developments that can change with unusually high frequency. However, it is also essential that e-managers distinguish between the few meaningful inputs and the many inputs that have limited significance.

- *Ability to sustain organizational change:* the e-world forces organizations to adapt well to change. With stunning swiftness a leading firm can lose its market position. For example, Cisco Systems went from dominating the router market to giving up 38 percent of that market to an upstart, Juniper Networks, in a mere 24 months. Effective e-managers monitor changes in their markets and adapt rapidly to stay ahead of these changes.

What about e-leadership?

Although the distinction between leadership and management has enjoyed significant popularity in some academic circles, it seems less relevant to me now. I think that whether you call it e-management or e-leadership, what matters is the ability to deliver consistently outstanding financial performance.

How do people use the Internet today?

From the perspective of traditional businesses using the Internet, I developed a model called the Web Applications Pyramid:

- At the bottom of this pyramid was a set of applications called Online Brochures. Online Brochures simply involved putting a company's marketing materials on the Web.
- In the middle of the pyramid was Front-Office Transactions which involved putting customer-facing activities such as placing an order on the Web while leaving back-office activities such as order fulfillment unchanged.
- At the top of the pyramid were Integrated Transactions in which a company actually linked its front-office and back-office systems and processes in a seamless fashion.

Most companies have developed online brochures; a smaller number have done some work with front-office transactions. While many companies are moving in the direction of integrated transactions, the peak of the pyramid has proven the most difficult to achieve, and few companies have actually gotten there. With the collapse of the dot.com bubble, there are many companies that will just decide that it is too hard to reach the peak and will give up. The few firms that persist and ultimately achieve integrated transactions are likely to enjoy a sustainable advantage over those which give up.

So what is the ultimate power of the Internet?

I have always been skeptical about the notion that the Internet will change everything. For industries in which the information content of a product is very high, the Internet has made significant change already. For example, there are very few retail stores in which consumers can buy boxed software. Now software companies tend to

enable people to download software to their computers. Companies such as Egghead Software have been wiped out by these changes.

On the other hand, industries like insurance remain essentially the same. Insurance agents take 25 percent of the premium dollar to distribute automobile insurance; commission is adding virtually no value. However, if consumers could access a Web site that compared auto insurance rates across all vendors and directed the consumers to the Web sites of the insurance companies with the lowest costs (thus removing insurance agents), such a Web site could siphon off most of the revenues from traditional insurance companies.

During the next five years, we will continue to feel the effects of the Internet bubble bursting, with more bankruptcies and more companies putting their technology initiatives on hold. Five to ten years from now, I believe that some new technology will come along with the power to transform society and the economy and unleash more of the

The few firms that persist and ultimately achieve integrated transactions are likely to enjoy a sustainable advantage over those which give up

economic power of the networked economy – creating a jolt of productivity and wealth creation so that what took place between 1995 and 2000 will pale in comparison. If there is one lesson to learn, it's that no technology, regardless of how profound its societal impact, can suspend the basic laws of economics over an extended period of time.

[jim collins]

master builder

a business mind fascinated by the triumph of great over good

Jim Collins (born 1958) is both a student and a teacher of enduring great companies. He has invested more than a decade in studying how companies become great, how they grow, and how they attain superior performance. His classic (with Jerry Porras), *Built to Last: Successful Habits of Visionary Companies* (1994, HarperCollins), was on the *BusinessWeek* bestseller list for 64 months, generating more than 70 printings and translations into 16 languages. The book has sold a million copies worldwide. He sees his latest work, *Good to Great* (2001, HarperCollins), as something of a prequel to this.

Collins started his research and teaching career at the Stanford Graduate School of Business, receiving the Distinguished Teaching Award in 1992. In 1995, he started a management laboratory in Boulder, Colorado, where he continues to conduct multi-year research projects and to work with senior executives from the public, private, and social sectors, including Starbucks Coffee, Merck, Sears, ARCO, Johns Hopkins Medical School, and the Boys and Girls Clubs of America.

The long-term research projects Jim undertakes help him to develop fundamental insights into business success, insights that he translates into his writing and consulting. Collins is also a dedicated rock climber. Why? "I climb every chance I get. It is a great way to clear my mind, to recharge. Rock climbing demands that you think

about nothing else. When you're 1500 feet up and it's just your hands and feet cling-ing to the rocks, you tend not to think about your New York publisher or anything else. You think about climbing – and the incredible joy of being alive. It's great. It's really great!"

For more information about Collins, visit *http://www.jimcollins.com*.

In this interview, Collins discusses how companies can be enduringly great – and how they make the leap from good to great.

Built to Last has been a big seller for almost a decade. Why?

I'm continuously surprised to see that the book keeps selling and sell-ing. I think we're pushing 1 million copies in print after some 64 months on the bestseller lists. Why does it continue to fascinate read-ers? My guess is that there are three reasons. First, Jerry and I talked about *the* corporate icons of the 20th century; we focussed on com-panies like IBM and Sony and Walt Disney. That draws a lot of people. Second, the quality of our research has obviously stood the test of time; the book uniquely looked at companies historically (to their roots) and comparatively (against their major competitors). Lastly, a lot of what's in that book are revelations about humans at work; we weren't afraid to have business findings mixed in with non-business, human findings.

How can we recognize what you call "core values" in an organization?

First of all, you don't need to have *explicit* core values. They don't have to be pretty, they can even be brutal, and they don't have to be human-itarian, although, in most cases, they are. The important thing is to know whether the values are believed in effectively. I recommend a test:

what values would you continue to hold even if the market, your industry, customers, and the media penalized you for holding them? Only such values are truly core.

So, a company should abandon clients and industries that prevent it from being faithful to its core values, even if profitable?

Exactly. It's a strong idea we stated on purpose to make the reader stop and say: "Did I read this right?" Most people think you need to adjust your values to your strategic needs. Great companies go the other way around: they discard any strategy – no matter how profitable it might be – if it would require actions inconsistent with the company's core values.

Customer intimacy is also a buzzword. It's a strategy concept, not a core value. The point is, there are no "right" core values

What about being an innovation leader?

Innovation depends on the company. If we're talking about Sony or 3M, I'll tell you clearly that innovation is a part of their core values, that they didn't read it in a book. It's something that's in their blood, written in their history. But there are other companies that don't value innovation, as is the case with Nordstrom, which doesn't prevent it from being a company with very strong values. Customer intimacy is also a buzzword. It's a strategy concept, not a core value. The point is, there are no "right" core values. The key question is not what are the "right" values but rather, what are the *authentic* values.

What about maximizing profits, often termed the essence of capitalism? Is that the purpose of a company?

Those who say it is are wrong. I am not a socialist, or the first to say it. In 1954, Peter Drucker, whom I most admire, wrote that maximizing profits is not a reason to exist for business. It is anti-social and immoral. A company doesn't exist to maximize its shareholders' or business owners' profits. Of course it will have to worry about earning profits and being profitable – that is the blood, oxygen, and nourishment of the company – but it has to have a deeper purpose. The expression "maximizing profits" is an ideological substitute for the need to find a purpose, something that is sometimes very difficult.

How is it possible to build a visionary organization without a charismatic leader? Business gurus have been trying to sell us the opposite for years.

These gurus are completely wrong. I can give you a listing of 20 world-class companies which don't have a charismatic leader. Let me ask you

this: where have all these mentors taken this idea of charisma from? For me, it is just a 20th-century version, for the management field, of what the 15th century tried while evoking God's name for everything. Charismatic leadership is one of the success factors, but there are others. Simplistic, all-purpose answers have to be discarded, like the charismatic leadership one.

So, are there some basic rules for becoming a *Built to Last* enterprise?

First, every company needs to have a core ideology – this is the first component of vision. It is not made like a cosmetic, or copied. It has to be discovered. Having a core ideology means having both core values and core purposes. They are something that remain throughout time.

Then, it is necessary to have a vision of the future, which means defining ambitious goals for the next 10–30 years. They don't have to be 100 percent manageable; maybe they just have a 50–70 percent probability of success. But they'll only have impact if they're described in a lively way, if the images picturing them are clear and motivating enough, if there is passion and conviction.

Lastly, aligning vision and implementation is essential: building a company requires 1 percent of vision (without it nothing matters) and 99 percent of alignment with implementation. Vision provides the context, but alignment allows anyone to understand what the company is about and where it is headed, without having to read papers or brochures, or listening to "top management" speeches. All you have to do is look at the operations and actions.

Your new work is *Good to Great*. Do you see that as a sequel?

Actually, I see it as more of a prequel. Ideally, you should read *Good to Great* before *Built to Last*. We didn't know it at the time, but the two books, combined, tell the story about how a new company can become a good company, then a great one, then one that is an enduring, visionary company.

But you see "good" as the enemy of great. Why?

Good is the enemy of great. Society doesn't have great schools because we have good schools; we don't have great government because we have good government; and we don't have that many great companies because too many are simply good. Ultimately, it's sad but true that many people don't have great lives because they're willing to settle for good lives. To be a great company, you have to adhere to relentlessly stiff standards. You have to stop accepting good-enough behaviors and performance. One of the major findings in the new book is that what companies and managers *stop* doing is infinitely more important than what's on their "To Do" list.

Is the "greatness gene" embedded in all companies, managers, employees?

Any company – *any* company – and I mean *any* organization, can become a great one. That was truly one of my own epiphanies in the past decade. I feel that we learned exactly how good companies become great ones. But the people inside a good company, starting with the leaders, have to commit – and stay committed.

[arie de geus]

organizational biologist

a business mind who has dug deep into "the living company"

The Dutchman Arie de Geus is considered the father of "the learning organization," a management buzzword of the 1980s which emerged into the established discipline of knowledge management.

De Geus made his mark by urging managers to look at companies through "biology lenses," not from the standard management points of view. Such a radical idea was honed into a full-length book, *The Living Company* (1997, Harvard Business School Press), which earned a "best book" citation from the *Financial Times* and a "most innovative" award by Booz-Allen & Hamilton. In the book, de Geus explores why certain companies (and only a few) endure for decades and centuries when most others fade away.

De Geus shaped his views on companies during a long career at Royal Dutch/Shell, where he was the coordinator of the most important think-tank of Shell, the group which focussed on strategic planning. There, de Geus became a proponent of managing organizations and change via scenario planning.

He is a member of the direction of the Center for Organizational Learning of the Sloan School of Management of MIT, and of Nijenrode Learning Centre of Nijenrode University, and The Netherlands Business School in Holland. He is also a founding

member of Global Business Network and visiting teacher at the London Business School. He is one of the founding members of the Society for Organizational Learning (SOL). Since his retirement from Shell in 1989, de Geus has headed an advisory group to the World Bank and consults with government and private institutions.

In this interview, de Geus explores what a learning organization is and is not – and why the distinction is important.

The language of business traditionally has been economics. You've tried to change that, haven't you?

That is because companies have become trapped in the prison of economic language, which is why so many companies suffer premature deaths. Said differently, companies tend to die early because their leaders and executives concentrate on production and profit, and forget that the corporation is an institution – that it is a community of human beings that should be in business to survive, and not to die after a while. Biology, definitively, has a more appropriate language than economics.

How did you arrive at this conclusion?

When I was at Shell, in 1983, we decided to conduct a study of corporate longevity. In that investigation we examined 27 well-documented cases of long-lived organizations. Some came from the 13th and 17th centuries, like Stora created in Sweden, Sumitomo and Mitsui in Japan. More than ten were born in the early 19th century. Our question was: how could these companies have lived so long? How was that possible? Especially given our points of contrast. For example, we found that of the 500 companies on the *Fortune* magazine list of 1970, one-third had disappeared 13 years later because of takeovers, fusion, or liquidation.

We found this terrible statistic: on average, corporate life expectancy is less than 20 years. Recently, a student updated this Shell study and found that the average life expectancy of an organization is twelve-and-a-half years. What this means is that the companies die in their teens, in their prime. That represents the liquidation of an enormous potential – and society will pay a dear price for that.

How did the success stories manage to survive against such odds?

Because they behaved like living species. It is not so far-fetched to view our institutions as central, rather than peripheral, to human survival. In the end, it is through organizations that humans also survive. And the secret of that perpetuation is to keep in harmony with the surrounding world. That is a learning process. It means that the company is open to the outside world, that it pays attention to what happens and reflects about what that means, what it implies. In doing so, organizational growth and survival become analogous to human growth and survival. It is about adaptation. That is the essence of learning. With the learning organization it is the same.

What are these long-lived organizations doing right?

The average human centigenarian advocates a life of abstinence, caution, and moderation, and so it is with companies. The Royal Dutch/Shell team identified four key characteristics: The long-lived were:

- *sensitive* to their environment;
- *cohesive*, with a strong sense of identity;
- *tolerant*; and
- financially *conservative*.

One important way to look at these findings is to realize that there is more to companies – and to longevity – than mere money making. Capital is no longer king; the skills, capabilities, and knowledge of people are. The corollary from this is that a successful company is one that can learn effectively. Learning is tomorrow's capital. And learning means being prepared to accept continuous change.

Most organizations are not demonstrating this capacity now?

Just look at the past 20 years of the global corporate story. It is a tale of discard rather than recycle. The "wisdom" of the past has been largely reengineered away, rather than appreciated and utilized. The mindset seems to be that the future lies in starting over with fresh faces – a clean sheet of paper, so to speak. But what about the loss of human potential, experience, and loyalty? How exactly is this mindset going to lead to a new, more secure corporate future?

The "wisdom" of the past has been largely reengineered away, rather than appreciated and utilized

Are we ready to make this move? Have we become a knowledge society?

A quiet revolution has taken place in modern businesses over the past 50 years. The outward signs of this revolution are the advent of many diverse, fast-growing businesses which do not employ much capital, or none at all – they only employ people! They are the Microsofts, the law firms, the international auditing and consulting firms, the EDSs, ServiceMasters, and financial service companies of the world. In these companies, there is no capital to be optimized, and their share of capital (if there is any) is only the key to power, not the source of their existence. These brain-rich, asset-poor companies are the engines of progress and economic growth in modern society.

The management challenges of such a company are significant, are they not?

To manage such organizations successfully requires a different mindset and different methods from their managers than were necessary in the traditional, pre-revolution company. In these modern companies, it is clearly visible to everybody who wants to look that Peter Drucker's "knowledge society" has arrived. In such companies, management knows that the only sustainable competitive advantage is the ability to learn faster than the competition. The revolution which created the knowledge society demands that leaders be thinking about how to convert from machinists to coaches, mentors, and stewards.

Explain what that means.

Managing a company for fast, high-quality knowledge creation and application is a different matter from managing the asset-rich company of half a century ago. The latter companies were like machines – their

managers were machinists. Machinists wanted their machines to perform according to predetermined design specifications. Control and the prevention of surprises were what these leaders needed to think about. Those who labored, a necessary evil, were but the hands attached to the machines. But today, even in these asset-rich companies, the revolution is playing out. The manufacture of one motorcar today costs much less in labor, capital, and energy than 50 years ago. The only factor that has increased is the amount of knowledge and ideas that have gone into the design of that motorcar and of the manufacturing processes to produce it. In other words, asset-rich companies are also more and more dependent for their success as a business on their ability to produce better ideas faster than their competitors. People – and their relationships with the company – have become the key to success.

What is the management alternative to traditional process control?

In a knowledge-dependent company, leaders must be thinking about creating space and freedom in their organizations – the antithesis of control and predetermined outcomes. They must be thinking about developing the potential of the individual members of their organization. In such companies, it is well understood that the ultimate potential of the organization is directly related to the extent that the individual members are encouraged to develop their potential. Beyond that, leaders must be thinking constantly about who their possible successors will be, in order to create an organization that is continuous over time. That kind of leadership requires courage based on trust. Continuity in the organization and a clearly demonstrated interest in the development of the individual members are basic conditions for the high levels of trust that the learning organization requires.

Do such ideas stand a chance with the "virtual organizations" of the new digital economy?

The digital economy, in my opinion, has put the emphasis in the wrong place. The essential piece is the knowledge; digital is the tool. I don't think that the virtual nets are enough to keep the communities of people. People have to meet alive, regularly. That kind of communication, largely informal, makes the organization click. It is what gives it life and what makes it an interesting and fulfilling place for people to spend their time. The expression "virtual organization" may be misleading.

[peter drucker]

vanguard historian

a business mind steeped in the past who has sagely predicted the future

Peter Drucker (born 1909, in Austria) has been described as "the world's most important and influential management thinker … a guru, an international legend, and business icon." The author of 29 books, including classics like *Concept of the Corporation* (1946, John Day), *The Practice of Management* (1954, Harper & Row), and *The Age of Discontinuity* (1969, Heinemann), he has received 19 honorary degrees from universities in the US, Belgium, Great Britain, Japan, Spain, and Switzerland – and orders from the governments of Austria and Japan. Drucker is in his 30th year on the faculty of Claremont Graduate University, which named its management center in his honor.

Shortly after Jack Welch became CEO of General Electric in 1980, he met with Drucker. At that meeting, Drucker asked Welch a big question: "If you weren't already in this business, would you choose to get into it now?" Welch's reaction: "You could write a book and not learn as much as you would from that question." The question spurred Welch to reshape the strategy for all GE: if it could not be No. 1 or No. 2 in a market, Welch sold it.

Now in his nineties, Drucker still teaches and consults. He is the honorary chairman of the Peter F. Drucker Foundation for Non-Profit Management. Despite the fact that he rarely travels, he can still be called the greatest influencer of management thinking in the world today. For more information, see *http://www.cgu.edu/faculty/druckerp.html*.

In this interview, Drucker reveals his grasp of historical trends and how those trends, when mixed with his observations of present-day happenings, can often become a prescient view of what tomorrow will yield for the business world.

What is "capitalism" today, considering the surge of a knowledge society and the digital economy?

There are two things which cannot be mixed. One is capitalism, the other is markets. Markets are not perfect, but they work, and nothing until now has worked better. Capitalism, on the other hand, is not what it used to be. There have been great structural changes during the 20th century. The first was a shift of power from the old "captain of industry" to the capital providers (the financial people), another was the advent of the organization as a new social institution we all need to work for, and finally the confirmation of the knowledge worker who owns the "property" of the production process, his knowledge.

But isn't financial capitalism more of the same?

That is not the point. The financial capitalism Rudolf Hilferding (the early 20th century German economist and politician) talked about at the beginning of the 20th century completely changed the economy of that time and, later, the same happened with the "invisible revolution" I foresaw in 1975, with the growth of mutual funds, which ultimately became, in the United States, the major providers of capital. This most recent financial revolution caused the situation today, where mutual funds own 40 percent of public companies. And who are those funds? Millions of anonymous investors, people worried about getting some complement for their retirement.

How are knowledge workers "ruining" capitalism?

With the knowledge worker, the issue of ownership of the production process has been inverted. He now owns the production process which is his own knowledge. The "alienation" the Marxists fought doesn't make sense any more for the people who own knowledge, mostly a high and specialized knowledge. The manual workers of capitalism did not have this ownership, but they had a great deal of experience, which only had an economic value in the place they worked, it wasn't "portable." Now knowledge is completely portable and the knowledge worker is not just one more "asset," in the traditional meaning of the word. He cannot be bought or sold.

Big is out of fashion, "small is beautiful" is back: is that the new message again?

That is not what I'm saying. The organization may be small and deal with the "big" issue through alliances and relationship management. I think alliances will be the major challenge of the future. They're a new way of organizing. And not only for new businesses but also for mature industries. Fifty years ago, when I wrote *Concept of the Corporation*, it was not that way. The way, then, was getting fat, being big just for the sake of it. Big today only means more problems. Nowadays, you have to be a partner and not a "boss." But it is difficult to learn to be a partner. It's a democratic relationship. I have also been saying that the organization is not limited to the business world. I've been trying to show the coming of the so-called "third industry," made of non-profit organizations and public service, as incubators of independence and diversity, as keepers of values and a source of leadership and citizenship in the civil society.

How would you then rate the frenzy of mergers and acquisitions creating mega-organizations?

They are not the solution. They make some sense if we see them as purely defensive in industries and sectors declining steadily. See the case of the car industry, or retail banking and traditional investments, the latter facing the shock of new financial services coming from places never dreamed of. There are new realities in the use of money and knowledge. Even the traditional financial community has not been aware of these new realities. A lot of banks are 150 years old; and, believe me, I know, being a veteran of the financial world as I am, where I started in Frankfurt (shortly before the 1929 crash) and then in London – the men now behind the great giants of the straightforward financial world don't understand a thing about management.

Nowadays, you have to be a partner and not a "boss." But it is difficult to learn to be a partner. It's a democratic relationship

not a

They don't understand a thing?

They don't! You have to show them what is today's basic philosophy of management. Today's business is not money, but information. Attracting talent is a true art. Keeping the right people is a priority, recruiting them well is essential, having their motivation is fundamental, making the knowledge workers productive is the greatest challenge of management for the next century, because competition is made today through people and a good management strategic design. The only possible advantage the developed countries will have is a supply of prepared people, educated and trained to work on a knowledge basis. We are living in a period of profound transition.

Your first book was published some 60 years ago. Where is management today?

I see four great changes. First, the end of orthodoxy in the management principle as a way of organizing and managing people. The idea of the Frenchman Henri Fayol, at the beginning of the 20th century, that there was only one single "correct" type of organization, is not useful any more. Today we don't believe that. The organization is not some-

"boss"

thing by itself: it's a tool. The second big change relates to the shift of the gravity center in the equation of the "information technologies," with the weight of the "T" from technologies shifting to the "I" from information. Broadly speaking, people tend to look "technocratically" at the information society, thinking about computers and the Internet as "technology" tools. But a new information revolution is under way. However, it is not mainly a revolution in technology, machines, techniques, software, speed. It's a concept revolution. Not understanding this is why many people in top management positions continue to face IT as data processing, instead of understanding that it is a source of information and knowledge, leading to new and different issues, new and different strategies.

Back to the changes I foresee. The third one is a return to "casual" times of turbulence.

Casual?

My friend, ongoing stability is the exception in history! The problem is that the great majority of people cannot adapt to this return of history to its "normal" course...of turbulence.

And the fourth great change?

The understanding that the growth areas of the 20th century in developed countries were not linked to the business world. There were others: governments, liberal professions, health, education, areas where good management is dramatically lacking. And I think that the most promising area in the next century will be the non-profit social industry.

You have said that the challenge of challenges is demographics. What should we be expecting?

It is another structural change, not essentially "economic." And it is probably the most important new reality, without precedent, in history. As you know, the birth rate has fallen greatly in most developed countries. It shows dramatically in Europe, which started this path that will culminate in a collective suicide at the end of the 21st century if the present collapse of the birth rate keeps on. At the same time, the weight of the older people is growing. We will watch, during the next century, as a dramatic shift unfolds, with older people overcoming by far young people.

What will this "white-haired revolution" mean for society and economy?

One of the challenges will be using these retired people, who are in a perfect physical and mental condition, making them useful to the society. It is important to learn how to work with older people; it could be an enormous competitive advantage. I even believe that, in the next 20 or 30 years, the age of retirement in the developed countries will have to be higher. Or at least, retirement will not mean coming out of the working world. Working relationships will probably become very heterogeneous and increasingly flexible.

[leif edvinsson]

intellectual capitalist

a business mind sensitive to a company's "intangible assets"

While many corporate annual reports contain platitudes such as "our people and their knowledge and skills are our most valuable assets," Leif Edvinsson (born 1946, in Sweden) was the first person to try to quantify the value of a company's *intellectual capital*. As the former vice president and the world's first "director of intellectual capital" (appointed in 1991) at Skandia, Sweden's largest financial services company, Edvinsson oversaw the creation of the world's first intellectual capital annual report.

In addition to his years at Skandia, Edvinsson was formerly senior vice president for training and development at Sweden's S-E Bank and chairman of Consultus AB, a Stockholm-based consulting firm. He has also served as a special adviser on service trade to the Swedish Cabinet, as a special adviser to the United Nations International Trade Center, and is a co-founder of the Swedish Coalition of Service Industries.

Edvinsson is the co-author, with Michael Malone, of *Intellectual Capital: Realizing Your Company's True Value by Finding its Hidden Brainpower* (1997, HarperBusiness). This book has been widely praised as the best resource on how to recognize the value of a company's intellectual assets which, Edvinsson argues, can far

exceed the value of its physical assets. His latest book is *Corporate Longitude* (2002, Financial Times/Prentice Hall).

In March 1998, he won the prestigious "Brain of the Year" award and, in 2000, was included in the list of the "20 Most Admired Knowledge Leaders" in the world. Currently, he heads his own IC-prototyping firm, Universal Networking Intellectual Capital (*www.unic.net*), based in Stockholm.

In this interview, Edvinsson discusses how the intangible assets of an enterprise can be worth substantially more than its capital equipment.

You often mention the importance of looking backward to better see forward. Why?

We won't understand the future without knowing and appreciating the past. The past offers us our perspective. There's a proverb which runs

It's not only the past that has been neglected as a source of learning. Traditionally we have been very poor at seeing the present evolving with any degree of accuracy

something like "We can't know where we are going if we don't know where we have been," and I think that largely holds true. Intellectual capital can be abbreviated as IC, I see is the future…with all its potential.

What about *where we are now?*

It's not only the past that has been neglected as a source of learning. Traditionally we have been very poor at seeing the present evolving with any degree of accuracy. In the mid-1950s, Peter Drucker predicted there would be 10–12 million college students in the US in 20 years' time. This was not guesswork. He simply combined two facts: increased birth rates and rising percentages of young people entering college. Universities rejected Drucker's forecasts and only a few prepared for massively increased numbers. There are countless other similar cases. We have to refine what we see, think, and feel now and transform it into actions to shape the future. What I call *the future* is 14 seconds down the road. Grasp it now. Grasp the potential, otherwise it quickly becomes a liability.

How do you confront skepticism about intellectual capital and knowledge management?

Knowledge management is only a fraction of intellectual capital. Knowledge management is about the storage, transfer, and migration of knowledge. It treats knowledge as an object, like a book in a library. Intellectual capital is concerned with the future earnings potential of the organization. IC is about cultivation of the living enterprise.

It puts a price on a company's staff?

This is still a common reaction from a major proportion of people. They see intellectual capital simply as the value of the staff and human cap-

ital in the company. But there's much more to it than that. Intellectual capital is a combination of human capital – the brains, skills, insights, and potential of those in an organization – and structural capital – things like the resources wrapped up in customers, processes, databases, brands, and systems. It is the ability to transform knowledge and intangible assets into wealth-creating resources, by multiplying human capital with structural capital. This is the IC multiplier effect that is actually exponential in its potential.

Isn't that intangibility something companies struggle with?

For some companies, like America Online and Microsoft, around 90 percent of their market capitalization value lies in intangibles, which are hard to visualize and therefore often hard to comprehend. Therefore we need to start to visualize it by both words and numbers, i.e. story telling and measurements. But what if we have been measuring the wrong things for decades and decades? And what if we've been measuring them in ways which present only partial truths? Such as historical cost accounting, instead of future potential and opportunity costs.

So measuring intangibles is more truthful?

The ultimate perspective is that the power of these intangibles is growing. Baruch Lev of Stern University in New York has examined American investment patterns. According to Baruch, back in 1929 around 70 percent of American investment went into tangible goods and some 30 percent into intangibles. Investors of that time backed "things." By 1990 the pattern was inverted. Now, intangible investments dominate. Things like R&D, education, and competencies, IT software, and the Internet. But what about the return on these intangible investments, i.e. the efficiency?

This is not just an American thing. On average, more than 10 percent of gross domestic product (GDP) in OECD (Organization for Economic Co-operation and Development) countries is estimated to go into intangibles. For countries like Sweden this input is calculated to be more than 20 percent of GDP. What you can't see is now driving the economies of the world. The intellectual capital of nations is the new wealth of nations. Capital is not just financial; capital is anything which adds new wealth. Period.

Is the new economy an intangible economy?

There is a lot of talk of the new economy. I'm not sure that "new" is the right adjective. After all, today's economy is always new. Things move on. Perhaps it is more useful to regard it as a new sphere for value creation, an intangible sphere or intellectual capital sphere, actually a lateral sphere. This requires genuinely new ways of looking at things, of expressing what we see and experience, and new ways of quantifying and measuring. That's where the newness lies. It is a new perspective – back to perspective again – and the right description might be knowledge economics.

How are traditional accounting practices unprepared for knowledge economics?

Traditional accounting misses so much. The resignation of a vital person will be accounted as a profit contribution, as it reduces the cost, and will not even be reported in the accounts unless they are the CEO. Yet we all know that individuals can hold huge amounts of power – knowledge power – in today's organizations. If a top software developer leaves a company, even a company as big as Microsoft, it is significant. Nor do accountants take customers into consideration. If a key account is lost, it is not mentioned. Indeed, not only do standard accounts tell

a partial story, they tell one which is written in a foreign language. How many people really understand the meaning of historical cost accounting such as "return on adjusted net asset value"? Not many I think. Often it is only the most attentive board member who can decipher all the footnotes and comments which cover all sorts of dark secrets. Accounting is essentially a knowledge tool, a kind of intelligence, or nerve system of the enterprise. Therefore it is essential to start to adapt the signal system to the new reality of the tremendous investments in intangibles.

What else are we missing?

Intelligence indicators. Take market share, one of the indicators with which companies have become preoccupied. They measure it with great enthusiasm and dedicate resources to making sure they know exactly how they are performing along this single parameter. But,

How many people really understand the meaning of historical cost accounting such as "return on adjusted net asset value"? Not many I think

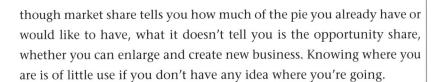

though market share tells you how much of the pie you already have or would like to have, what it doesn't tell you is the opportunity share, whether you can enlarge and create new business. Knowing where you are is of little use if you don't have any idea where you're going.

Is opportunity share better to focus on than market share?

Yes. Look at what we did at Skandia. As an insurance company it could have continued to concentrate on market share. Fortunately, the company realized that growth comes from vigorously seeking out new market opportunities rather than obsessing over its share of markets it was already in. The future never lies in the present. So we transformed Skandia from an old insurance company into an innovative global financial service organization and Fortune 500 company.

What have been the benefits to Skandia of following the intellectual capital route?

There could be a figure in dollars and cents – in excess of $15 billion. But the effect was more profound than that. Managing intellectual capital nourished new thinking, innovation, and new perspectives. Another mind-set, a mind compass for the future.

But aren't the measures we use to understand intangibles as vague and intangible as what they attempt to measure?

No. Remember that measures we regularly use such as IQ, GDP, p/e and the like are crude and fuzzy to work with. We understand GNP (gross national product), but do we really believe that it is all that precise a measure? Geometry can be valuable and useful now and then, even

though there are no infinite straight lines or perfect circles. The tools developed at Skandia do not value intellectual capital correctly to five decimal points. They account for the value evolution of intangible assets. Most importantly, they supply a balance by charting a course from yesterday to tomorrow. We found that the key ratios this tool created allowed us to detect flaws which tended to be camouflaged by traditional accounting systems. Measurement could then become a me-assuring system.

The changes you're suggesting will alter both the managerial job and environment, right?

Of course. And at a personal level things will change also. The most rapidly growing disease in Sweden is burn-out or brain stress. While it takes some weeks to chemically treat cancer, burn-out takes much longer to treat. This is not just a Swedish problem. In Japan there is *karoshi* – death by overwork – and working hours in the US are significantly higher than those in Europe. We are working harder rather than smarter. So the knowledge leader has to pay much more attention to knowledge care.

The challenge, then, of intellectual capital includes the health of the knowledge worker?

We can call it knowledge care. One good example of this is to replace offices with another meeting type or knowledge arena, such as a knowledge café. We need to have space to clear our heads to seize our own opportunities. In years gone by, people took the waters in search of physical restoration. Now, we need mental spas, places where we can renew ourselves and our minds. The opportunity cost of not seizing this potential is enormous. This is brain economics – caring for the knowledge potential.

What is the key question you ask when you go into a company?

Where is your intellectual capital and how efficient is it?

What question would you like to ask the managers of the world?

How will we increase the efficiency of our intellectual capital investments to achieve greater wealth creation for future generations?

[sumantra ghoshal]

knowledge miner

a business mind who *knows* that knowledge is power in the marketplace

Sumantra Ghoshal (born 1948, in India) is the founding dean of the new Indian School of Business in Hyderabad, a new venture jointly sponsored by the Wharton School at the University of Philadelphia, the Kellogg School of Business at Northwestern University, and the London Business School. Ghoshal also holds the Robert P. Bauman Chair in Strategic Leadership at the London Business School, where he is a member of the strategy and international management faculty. He has previously taught at INSEAD and MIT's Sloan School of Management.

Described by *The Economist* as a Euroguru, Ghoshal's research focusses on strategic, organizational, and managerial issues confronting large, global companies. He has published nine books, more than 50 articles, and several award-winning case studies. *Managing Across Borders: The Transnational Solution* (1989, Harvard Business School Press), a book he co-authored with Christopher Bartlett, has been listed by the *Financial Times* as one of the 50 most influential management books of the 20th century and has been translated into nine languages.

The Differentiated Network: Organizing the Multinational Corporation for Value Creation, co-authored with Nitin Nohria, won the George Terry Book Award in 1997, and *The Individualized Corporation* (1997, Harvard Business School Press), co-authored with Christopher Bartlett, won the Ignor Ansoff Award in 1997, and has been translated into seven languages. Ghoshal's latest book, *Managing Radical Change: What Indian Companies Must Do to Become Worldclass* (2000, Penguin: India), won the Management Book of the Year award in India in 2000.

More about Ghoshal can be found at *http://www.sumantraghoshal.com*.

In this interview, Ghoshal points out how knowledge can be both a fascinating subject to talk about, and critically important for modern management.

Critics have suggested that knowledge management (KM) was a big idea that failed to deliver.

To say knowledge management hasn't delivered the goods is an exaggeration. But overall, organizations haven't reaped the benefits predicted. Many companies initially saw knowledge management as a technical task and handed it over to their IT people, who went away and created sophisticated IT systems. But it's really a social, not a technological, issue. Where it has been effective it is because much more attention has been paid to the human dimension – the social, emotional, and relational contexts.

You're saying that KM goes beyond codifying and compiling?

In the first rush of enthusiasm for KM, many organizations largely missed the point that a substantial amount of knowledge in any organization is tacit and cannot be written down. Even when knowledge can be codified, there is no guarantee that useful knowledge will be identified and exploited. An example involving British Telecommunications

highlights the difficulties of practicing knowledge management. It came to light that for 14 years BT had been sitting on a US patent covering hyperlinks, one of the key building blocks of the World Wide Web. Despite KM initiatives, the patent, which was potentially worth millions, remained buried in a filing cabinet in the company's vaults along with thousands of other global patents.

How do you find tacit knowledge?

Companies must address human capital at a more profound level. Often we make the mistake of thinking of human capital as just knowledge. A second important aspect is social capital – networks and relationships. The third dimension is emotional capital – the ability and willingness to act.

Knowledge, relationships, and the willingness to act may call for dramatic cultural changes in many organizations. Correct?

There is no solution other than a trust-based culture. It's not so much "I have this knowledge which I give to you," it's more "how do you shape questioning and frame learning?" Those are cultural considerations. At BP, for example, a quarter of the knowledge management budget is spent on coaching people. If you look at Skandia, it is trying to institutionalize questioning. What is special about the company is not the tools it uses but its attempts to embed curiosity in the culture.

Why curiosity?

Most companies have only scratched the surface of this bigger issue. The new source of competitive advantage is dreams and ambitions. Today we are in the world of the volunteer employee. People choose to invest their human capital in companies to get the best returns. They are mobile investors. The real challenge for KM lies in creating the context in which people will want to invest themselves and their knowledge in the company. That will require senior management to demonstrate its ability to obtain a good return for the individual.

This focus on the individual, and the uniquely human components of the organization, certainly calls organization structure and strategy into question.

William Whyte's *Organization Man* of the 1950s (1956, Simon & Schuster) is still the model organizational citizen for too many companies. But the philosophy of that day suggested that if strategy, structure, and related organizational systems were well defined, the rest – namely the individuals – was not important. That model is obsolete. It is necessary to change the focus from the organization to the individual. That is a fundamental and necessary shift.

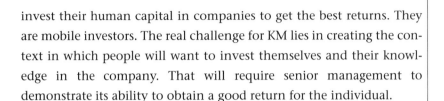

The new source of competitive advantage is dreams and ambitions

Is this part of a "managerial revolution" of the 21st century?

That is an attractive way of exaggerating the issue. In the 20th century there were great innovations in management. The greatest one, without any doubt, was Alfred Sloan's organization of General Motors. Until the 1980s and 1990s all corporations were organized functionally – Sloan's vision. That was what was meant by "organization" and "corporation." But now it is clear that the model has reached its limits. The 21st century is a whole new ball game than Sloan's time.

Sloan's ideas were awfully effective.

That is very true. Let's go back in history so that we can understand what Sloan did and what is done now. In the 1920s and 1930s the big corporations were full of complicated problems – they were too big and terribly complex. That's when Sloan invented the "multi-division structure," which was not only a structure, it was also a new management philosophy. That made possible the diversifying of products and businesses, and globalization. All the big corporations that have survived till today are children of Sloan's invention. In the 1980s, in my opinion, they peaked, and another innovation became necessary. Enter Percy Barnevik of ABB and Jack Welch of General Electric. These two are the Sloan and Du Pont of today.

If "structure follows strategy" is not the correct blueprint for success, what is?

All those polemics surrounding structure and strategy are children and grandchildren of the same model created by Sloan that we have talked about. They are two faces of the same coin. It is time to override this contradiction. We now need to view the successful corporation as defined by its purpose, by its processes, and by its people. Let's end that old debate about strategy-structure and vice versa. "Strategy" needs to inspire creativity and individual initiative. That is fundamental in today's corporation. Organizational processes need to facilitate the innovation and renovation necessary to permanently reshape companies. People and processes are part of the same strategic effort.

Is this a "strategic revolution," in the sense that we've read about in many books?

I am suggesting changing the conditions, the ambience, the environment, the "smell of the place" so that revolutionary strategy may emerge.

Managers are actors at three levels, all necessary: in the front line (as entrepreneurs), in the middle (as facilitators and integrators), and at the top (as institution builders)

In this new organization, is there a place for middle managers or are they condemned to death?

In no way is that position in peril! It would be completely wrong, a catastrophe. Many corporations made that mistake in the last decades marked by downsizing frenzy. Managers are actors at three levels, all necessary: in the front line (as entrepreneurs), in the middle (as facilitators and integrators), and at the top (as institution builders). The middle role is vital; it is like a glue. There is no death but a redefinition of roles.

Do you think that Europe will be producing examples of this new corporate model, introducing the emergence of a new group of European thinkers with world importance?

History will tell. But there are several examples that come to mind immediately: ABB, BP, Nokia. Or look at what IKEA had done in the furniture business, or ISS in the cleaning area. So I think the answer is yes.

Making big or "revolutionary" changes is tough for a small company, and tougher for a large organization.

No doubt about that. So the process needs to be done incrementally. The necessary steps include starting by rationalizing and creating an entrepreneurial spirit (a giant task in itself), fostering and rewarding the new behaviors, and then working to revitalize the organization, changing the processes and developing synergy that actually creates an auto-renovation dynamic.

So, with some work, paraphrasing Rosabeth Moss Kanter, an elephant really can learn the change dance?

Consider one final example: the transmission and distribution division of Westinghouse, purchased by ABB in 1989. A radical transformation occurred with exactly the same management team, but with a new philosophy and a new enthusiasm. I believe in this: the essential problem is not to change people, the real problem is to create a new atmosphere, what we call "the smell of the place." What ABB did in that Westinghouse division was to create a new smell, instead of behaving like an invasion army. It did not follow the classical trend in the takeover, and the results speak for themselves.

[beverly goldberg]

social progressive

a business mind who ties business leadership to social progress

After years at The Century Foundation (formerly The Twentieth Century Fund), a New York-based think-tank focussed on the impact of economic, social, political, and demographic events, it is not surprising that when Beverly Goldberg (born 1940) began to study business, she examined everything from the executive suite to the shop floor.

Her analyses of the way corporations do (and should!) work, as set forth in her major books – *Dynamic Planning: The Art of Managing Beyond Tomorrow* (1994, Oxford University Publishing) and *Corporation on a Tightrope: Balancing Leadership, Governance, and Technology* (1996, OUP) (both written with John Sifonis), *Overcoming High-Tech Anxiety: Thriving in a Wired World* (1999, Jossey-Bass), and *Age Works: What Corporate America Must Do to Survive the Graying of the Workforce* (2000, Free Press) – take a holistic view of the business world. *Business Week* praised *Age Works* as "a serious, carefully researched" book, noting that Goldberg "argues persuasively that companies must come up with a flexible work environment" if they are to continue to recruit and retain the best and brightest employees. She was also interviewed on the impact of changing demographics by *Harvard Business Review*.

In her editorials in major newspapers and in hundreds of radio interviews, Goldberg has explored the intersection of social and business issues and what they mean for future economic health. Her writings explore strategic and governance issues, the impacts of technology on corporate management and structure, the role of leadership (especially ethical leadership), and the need to adapt to demographic changes. Vice president of The Century Foundation, she can be reached via *http://www.tcf.org*.

In this interview, Goldberg discusses how business leaders can be profit-minded – and progressive thinkers.

Your book about corporations being on "a tightrope" was intriguing. Is the analogy still apt? How?

It remains even truer today. The point of *Corporation on a Tightrope* was that change now takes place so rapidly that managing a business in this day and age is a constant balancing act, one in which you have to be alert to every breeze that can push you off course, that can make it impossible for you to reach your goals. The book stressed the importance of adapting the three critical components of any organization – governance, leadership, and technology – to ensure that a company can change rapidly to meet shifts in the world economy, in the competitive environment, and in its own industrial sector, as well as deal with scientific and technological developments and changes in the markets for the goods and services it produces.

The book calls on companies to examine the kinds of boards they have, how responsibilities are assumed and accountability measures put in place, as well as their internal structures. It also asks leadership to accept that ethics are a critical component in determining the kind of culture an organization has, which is essential to attracting the best and

brightest workers in a highly competitive environment. And it focusses on the need to deal with the impacts of technology on every aspect of the business.

With change taking place ever more rapidly as a result of the speed of communications and of developments enabled by technology, the need to be alert to forces that can push an organization off balance is not likely to lessen. In the face of the constant churning that results, it is ever more important that organizations stay prepared to turn rapidly in response to developments. And it is even more critical that they ensure that they have a core workforce that can handle these changes, employees who understand that change is a norm and employees who are prepared to learn continuously. To do that, the organization's leadership must construct an environment in which trust and caring for employees are the norm.

In the face of the constant churning that results, it is ever more important that organizations stay prepared to turn rapidly in response to developments

Has leadership stepped up to deal with the difficulties you describe?

There is no *yes* or *no* answer. In many organizations, leadership has tried to respond to outside developments by making changes in one or another area. The problem is that the changes made often are not fully integrated into the organization as a whole; for example, technological strategies and structures and business strategies and structures are not aligned to ensure that everyone has the same critical success factors in mind as the organization forges ahead. In the case of the so-called new economy companies, the recent collapse of so many of them is evidence of a failure of their leaders to put in place governance structures and business models that work in the context of the old economy as well.

To what extent is your POV about the business world influenced by working in a New York think-tank?

It is influenced in every way. For example, among the issues The Century Foundation – which was established by Edward A. Filene in 1919 – is concerned with are domestic problems such as inequality and education. One of the things I've emphasized in all my writing is the need for corporations to work with employees to ensure that they are given access to constant retraining. I also stress the need to create flexible work structures, including job sharing, telecommuting, and staggered hours. However, it is critical that businesses do not use these flexible arrangements as a means to deny employees benefits such as health care and pension contributions.

Do you see the world of business and the concerns of society meshing as we enter a new century?

They have always meshed and will continue to do so. Filene was an enormously successful retailer (think of Filene's Department Stores, later Federated Stores) who truly believed that social progress and business progress were dependent on each other. He maintained that the healthier and better educated an employee, the more productive an employee. Like Henry Ford, he understood that workers were the consumers of his product and therefore had to be paid adequate wages.

In broader terms, in the years immediately following a great set of changes – the agricultural revolution, the industrial revolution, and, perhaps, the computer revolution – many people suffer from the displacements and waves of changes that occur. Once things settle down, however, the standard of living of the descendants of those who suffered from the turmoil brought by the changes dramatically improves.

Management ideas are great when they are holistic, that is, when they take every aspect of the enterprise into account instead of focussing on a single immediate problem

The improvements are not just in the availability of goods for everyone, but in such things as advances in medicine and education. The alleviation of social concerns thus comes about because of business.

What do you think makes a management idea great?

Management ideas are great when they are holistic, that is, when they take every aspect of the enterprise into account instead of focussing on a single immediate problem. I think many good ideas have been lost because they were jumped on as the "perfect solution" before they were tried and tested. Others survive, but only after many costly failures. For example, when business process reengineering was introduced, companies tried to apply it without changing their corporate culture, their management styles, their activities at every level. It took a number of years of false starts for the percentage of successful efforts to reach truly impressive levels.

What do you think will prove to be the most influential management idea of all time?

I don't think there is a single idea that will hold that title. Everything has a time and place. Great management ideas emerge to fit the time in which they evolve. I'd like to be able to say that the one exception is treating one's employees as valuable stakeholders in the enterprise. But even that makes me nervous because the robotic factory may one day be with us. Context is just too important to ignore.

You have written about the aging workforce. Is this a problem that really requires global management attention? Why did you choose to focus on it?

Demographics tell us that it is going to prove a major problem for business in the next two decades. Before the economic dip that took place in 2001, the effects of the combination of early retirement and a smaller generation entering the workforce were already being felt. The OECD was issuing warnings that, if labor participation by those over 55 did not increase by at least 25 percent, the world would not be able to maintain a constant total employment-to-population ratio from 2005 onward. The impact of the aging of the baby boomers, which is the cause of the problem, is already being felt in Western Europe, but Japan, Canada, and the United States are not far behind.

The idea of encouraging older workers to remain in the workforce should not be seen as a form of cruelty to the elderly. When 65 was set as the retirement age, most people died shortly after reaching their 65th year. Today life expectancy is far longer, and most people who reach 65 can expect to live another 15 or so years. Thanks to advances in medicine, people from 60 to 70 are much healthier than people that age were in the past. Moreover, they are going to have to finance a far lengthier retirement, so working a little longer makes sense. I was alerted to the size of the problem by work we were doing at The Century Foundation on social security, which is an issue the Foundation has dealt with since the Great Depression. Aware of the economic catastrophe facing widows with children and older people in the early 1930s, the Foundation supported much of the thinking and analysis that led to the nation's social security program.

Suppose you had an audience of thousands of managers in one spot and you could ask them one question. What would that question be?

What do you want to be remembered for? We are all concerned about our legacy, the way we will be thought about by those whose lives we touch. Answering that question should help managers realize that they are far more likely to be remembered for an example of ethical behavior, for standing up for someone not getting a fair deal, for helping someone on the path to success. It might also be interesting to ask them to think about what the most successful business people do with their gains – Andrew Carnegie endowed libraries, Henry Ford set up the Ford Foundation, Bill Gates's philanthropy is aimed at improving the health and learning of children. It all comes down to finding ways to make life better for others.

Do you see businesses succeeding in the 21st century for the same reasons (in the same way) businesses succeeded in the past 100 years?

That's a difficult question. Today, so much of business in the developed world is service related rather than manufacturing, a huge change since the first half of the 20th century. The addition of the Internet, which is still in its infancy when it comes to business, further complicates the picture. The average life of a major corporation is not much longer than the average life span of humans now – about 75 years. What will the new generation of businesses look like? What will it take for them to succeed? Time will tell, but my guess is that we are looking for evolutionary rather than revolutionary changes.

[daniel goleman]

eq advocate

a business mind who is willing to probe the emotions

Daniel Goleman (born 1946) is a name synonymous with "emotional intelligence" (EQ). His book, *Emotional Intelligence* (1997, Bantam), has more than 5 million copies in print and was on the *New York Times* bestseller list for 18 months. Similarly, his follow-up book, *Working With Emotional Intelligence* (1997, Bantam), became an immediate bestseller.

Goleman works with companies through the emotional intelligence practice of the Hay Group. He is also co-chairman of the Consortium for Social and Emotional Learning in the Workplace, based in the School of Professional Psychology at Rutgers University, which recommends best practices for developing emotional competence.

Goleman is both a clinical psychologist and a distinguished journalist. He has received two Pulitzer Prize nominations for his articles in the *New York Times*, a Career Achievement award for journalism from the American Psychological Association, and was elected a Fellow of the American Association for the Advancement of Science. To learn more about his work, log onto *http://eisglobal.com*.

In this interview, Goleman explains why it is critical to understand the emotional side of people, especially in the business world.

How did the concept of emotional intelligence originate?

While covering brain and behavior research for the *New York Times*, I became aware of how little correlation existed between intelligence tests and what it takes to be successful in life. Study after study showed that success had surprisingly little to do with IQ (intelligence quotient) – IQ accounting for only about 4–10 percent of the variance. On the other hand, the ability to handle one's emotions, deal with frustration, self-awareness, self-discipline, persistence, empathy, and being able to get along with people – skills we learn as children – did appear to matter a great deal.

Where did that realization lead?

Along with data on issues such as aggression in US schools, and the neurology of emotions, I compiled the research which became the book *Emotional Intelligence*. I've since gone on to explore the relationship between EQ and many facets of personal and professional effectiveness. Sadly, I have found that we ignore emotional competencies at our peril. It is unhealthy to do so. Children can, and should, be taught these abilities at school.

It seems almost counter-intuitive to look at the business world – a world defined by facts, analysis, data, and intellect – as driven more by emotional than non-emotional forces.

The emotional climate is more important to the success of an organization than previously recognized. In particular, the emotional dimension is critical in determining the effectiveness of leaders. In jobs where above-average IQ is a given, superior emotional capability gives leaders

an edge. At senior levels, emotional intelligence rather than rational intelligence marks out the true leader. And the best news is that emotional intelligence can be learned. My previous work had not focussed on leaders *per se*, but on people in jobs of all kinds. Leadership puts unique demands on people that makes how well they handle themselves and others of paramount importance. Leadership is the art of getting work done through other people: it's a relationship capability.

And EQ helps people manage relationships better?

There are four dimensions to EQ, and each one has an impact on how we interact with others. Don't think of EQ as beginning and ending in each person's head. Emotional intelligence affects how people conduct themselves among others.

All effective leaders learn to manage their emotions, especially the big three: anger, anxiety, and sadness

What is the first dimension?

Self-awareness. We seldom pay attention to what we feel. A stream of moods runs in parallel to our thoughts. This and previous emotional experiences provide a context for our decision making. The better we understand ourselves and our experiences, the better decisions we will make.

The second dimension?

Managing emotions. All effective leaders learn to manage their emotions, especially the big three: anger, anxiety, and sadness. But this isn't just a leadership skill. This is a decisive life skill. People need to learn how to recognize and manage their emotions.

And next?

The third dimension is *empathy* which is essential for motivating others. The root meaning of motive is the same as the root of emotion: to move. And, showing empathy refers to the ability to read emotions in others. Good motivators understand and care about others.

And the fourth dimension is…

Staying connected – managing relationships well. Emotions are contagious: there is an unseen transaction that passes between us in every interaction that makes us feel either a little better or a little worse. This "secret economy" holds the key to motivating the people we work with.

Most people would agree that leadership is less an attribute and more a relationship. Your argument is that the relationship called leadership has more to do with EQ than IQ. But doesn't IQ inform technical skills and workplace competencies – both leadership attributes?

> Workplace competencies based on emotional intelligence play a far greater role in star performance than do intellect or technical skill. Studies of outstanding performers in organizations show that about two-thirds of the abilities that set star performers apart in the leadership stakes are based on emotional intelligence; only one-third of the skills that distinguish star performers relate to raw intelligence (as measured by IQ) and technical expertise.

How can that be?

> Our emotions are hardwired into our being. The very architecture of the brain gives feelings priority over thought. In reality, it is impossible to entirely separate thought from emotion. We can be effective only when the two systems – our emotional brain and our thinking brain – work together. That working relationship, which encompasses most of what we do in life, is the essence of emotional intelligence.

Do the best-selling leadership books have it wrong?

> Part of the problem is that pontificating and hypotheses, rather than hard data, have generally been the currency of leadership theorists. This, it must be said, is usually true. The average book on leadership is more likely to feature Churchillian quotations than rigorous analysis of the behavior of leaders.

What has your research on behaviors shown?

Data from the Hay Group on more than 3000 executives has identified six separate leadership styles.

- Coercive leaders demand immediate compliance.
- Authoritative leaders mobilize people toward a vision.
- Affiliative leaders create emotional bonds and harmony.
- Democratic leaders build consensus through participation.
- Pacesetting leaders expect excellence and self-direction.
- And coaching leaders develop people for the future.

Is one style better, or more effective, than the others?

It would be more accurate to say that effective leaders need to apply different leadership styles in different situations. Today's coercive leader

Leaders who have mastered four or more styles, especially the authoritative, democratic, affiliative, and coaching strategies, have the best climate and business performance

may need to switch to coaching mode in the next meeting. Leaders who have mastered four or more styles, especially the authoritative, democratic, affiliative, and coaching strategies, have the best climate and business performance.

So leaders require a mix of pragmatism and mental agility?

That makes sense, of course, to survive the demands of internal organizational politics coupled with external markets, not to mention changes in the business world. Companies are reevaluating the leadership characteristics they require for the future. Some companies talk about an inward journey. Emotional intelligence is part of that redefinition.

Will heightened emotional intelligence contribute to the "bottom line"?

Many, many studies show the value of EQ as a human resource tool. Examples include studies by the US Air Force, which used EQ successfully to select recruiters, and saved $3 million annually; job performance studies which indicate that as much as two-thirds of the differences in productivity are due to emotional intelligence rather than technical skill or cognitive abilities; as well as studies done at L'Oreal, in insurance agencies, beverage firms, computer companies, furniture retailers, among senior executives and office clerks, and even cross-cultural studies of executives in Latin America, Germany, Japan, and the United States.

What is the basic conclusion drawn from the wealth of organization studies regarding EQ?

It is important to understand why emotional intelligence needs to be incorporated in our understanding of organizational effectiveness. Emotional intelligence is the foundation for competencies that matter in work effectiveness. Emotional intelligence allows a person to learn essential skills or competencies, such as initiative. Predicting job performance accurately depends on being able to measure these competencies.

[gary hamel]

business revolutionary

a business mind who's not afraid to overthrow the status quo

Gary Hamel (born 1954) has been called "the world's reigning strategy guru" by *The Economist*. Indeed, his non-linear thinking about business strategy calls for a radical innovation agenda in business, telling companies that they must continually reinvent themselves, not just at times of crisis. His landmark book, co-authored with C.K. Prahalad, *Competing for the Future* (1994, Harvard Business School Press), was *BusinessWeek's* book of the year in 1995.

He has also published nine articles in the *Harvard Business Review*, three of which won the prestigious McKinsey Prize for Excellence. His most recent book, *Leading the Revolution* (2000, Harvard Business School Press), calls for companies to throw aside their single-strategy business plans and instead develop a deeply embedded capability for continual, radical innovation.

Hamel has taught at both the University of Michigan Graduate School of Business Administration and the London Business School. He is a founder of Strategos, a firm dedicated to helping companies build high-performance innovation systems. He has given keynote speeches at the Microsoft CEO Forum, at the World Economic Forum, and at the Confederation of British Industry, and has been featured on CNN, CNBC, and the BBC.

Hamel dislikes the "Dilbert" cartoon strip and Dilbert's cynical views of management. He sees the need for visionary activists, not cynics, in business. "We need antidotes to Dilbert," says Hamel. For more on Hamel's thinking, visit *http://www.strategos.com*.

In this interview, Hamel focusses on the "revolutionary" business thinking for which he is now noted.

Is strategic planning as you describe it the end of strategic planning as written by Henry Mintzberg?

I wouldn't say so. Mintzberg's strategic planning brought very good things. But in my opinion, there is a fundamental difference between his thinking and what I call "business strategizing." To plan is not to create something new, and creating newness is what we need to do.

The objective of the revolutionary is to free the process from the tyranny of the past

What is creative strategizing?

Mostly it will take revolutionary thinking along a few key lines. First, strategic planning is not strategy. Planning and strategic formulations are very different things. Strategy is discovering and inventing, which makes strategy subversive, and the strategist a rule-breaker, or revolutionary. Second, the real barrier to strategic planning is generally at the top, not in the middle or at the bottom. The objective of the revolutionary is to free the process from the tyranny of the past. Its guardians are at the top. And third, you cannot expect to see the end at the start. The strategic formulation is a discovery process and a moment of invention. It is not selling to those in the middle and at the bottom something already defined by those at the top or from outsiders (the external consultants).

Where will this creativity come from?

Successful strategizing is dependent on four conditions in the organization:

- it is necessary to include new voices in the strategic formulation (if you always have the same panel, the conversation is repetitive);
- it is necessary to bring a new perspective;
- it is necessary to create strategic conversations about the future of the corporation;
- and it is necessary to have passion.

You're talking about a dramatically different perspective on strategizing. Yes?

We like to believe we can break strategy down to Five Forces or Seven Ss. But you can't. Strategy is extraordinarily emotional and demanding.

It is not a ritual or a once-a-year exercise, though that is what it has become. We have set the bar too low. As a result, managers are bogged down in the nitty-gritty of the present – spending less than 3 percent of their time looking to the future.

But hasn't this ritualistic approach created great wealth and formidable companies?

Basically, we see three kinds of companies. First are the rule makers, companies such as British Airways and Xerox. They are the aristocracy; well managed, consistently high achievers. Second are the rule takers, peasants who only keep what the lord doesn't want. This group typically have around 15 percent market share – such as Kodak in the copier business or Avis. Third are the rule breakers, industrial revolutionaries. These companies are creating the new wealth, and include the likes of Starbucks in the coffee business. Companies should be asking themselves, who is going to capture the new wealth in our industry?

What are the biggest differences between the three?

Simply put, corporations that are rule takers systematically focus on trying to catch the present market leaders, those that establish the laws – the rule makers – but never succeed in catching them. A lot of time gets lost in benchmarking that does not solve the problem. What is profitable is to be a rule breaker and reinvent the industry.

Do you think that a rule taker can change and become a subversive rule breaker?

Yes, it can make that transition. What is necessary is that the managers do not stay prisoners of that benchmarking mentality in relation to the rule makers of their industry, and so spend unwarranted time trying to

imitate those actual leaders. I would tell them to look outside their industry and discover new ideas. Instead of trying to be as good or even a little better than the leader, do another thing: reinvent the rules.

Do you think that a rule maker, used to market position and power, might actually want to become a rule breaker? For example, do you think that Microsoft will be able to make that transition?

I am not sure that Microsoft is going to transform itself into a rule breaker. I think that is the question they ask themselves there. Personally, I think that Microsoft is in a situation somehow similar to IBM 20 years ago. In recent years, Microsoft has not led in several areas of innovation in its industry – areas such as programming language for the Internet or virtual banking. But I do not underestimate Microsoft. It is clear that it is responding much quicker than IBM did in the 1980s.

Is it hard to keep from getting too cynical about management?

Complacency and cynicism are endemic. The *Dilbert* book on management is the bestselling business book of all time. It is cynical about management. Never has there been so much cynicism. It is only by challenging convention that change will happen. Taking risks, breaking the rules, and being a maverick have always been important, but today they are more crucial than ever. We live in a discontinuous world, one in which digitalization, deregulation, and globalization are profoundly reshaping the industrial landscape.

You're certainly not talking about tinkering around the edges, are you?

The primary agenda is to be the architect of industry transformation, not simply corporate transformation. Companies which view change as an internal matter are liable to be left behind. Instead they need to look outside of their industry boundaries. If you want to see the future coming, 80 percent of the learning will take place outside company boundaries. This is not something companies are very good at. Do you think that business process reengineering, which was also presented to us as revolutionary from the beginning of the 1990s, is becoming less revolutionary and more incremental? In reengineering there is a great difference between theory and practice. Theoretically, what Champy and Hammer said (in their 1993 book *Reengineering the Corporation*) is really revolutionary. In practice, what I have seen is really more incremental than paradigm breaking. Even if there are deep changes in the processes, that does not mean that you are reinventing the industry.

Companies which view change as an internal matter are liable to be left behind

Have corporations just about reached the limits of what incremental change can accomplish?

Over the past ten years, corporations have focussed mainly on operational improvement, in the field of restructuration, or even reengineering. That was important, it is true, because they were very much behind in terms of quality, cost, and customer service. Much of what was done was designed to "catch" the competition, the leaders of the market. Now there are corporations interested in another game, to go beyond incrementalism in being innovative.

But is there a real difference between incrementalism and innovation?

Applied correctly, there is all the difference in the world. In my opinion, the founding principle of strategy is the capacity and the willingness to challenge the existing beliefs about a given business. Reengineering forces us to challenge the processes, but not necessarily the convictions about the nature of that business. Incremental and continuous improvement is a necessity but will not guarantee competitive advantage to companies. In the long run, successful companies must have the processes, ideas, people, principles, and courage it takes to continually challenge their orthodoxies (the way they became successful the first time), look at what type of discontinuous change is happening in the world, and try to apply it to future customer benefits, and find ways to fundamentally reinvent their business model to avoid irrelevancy.

Will the revolution you call for survive the "new economy"?

The "new economy" is a fallacy. There is one economy. Those firms that can successfully implement radical new technologies like the Internet, which provide radical leaps in transparency, non-incremental reduction in channel costs, and new opportunities to fundamentally reinvent the ways customers are provided benefits, will continue to take advantage of technology. Those companies which use technology as their strategy, instead of as a means to implement some aspect of a technology, will continue to fail, as was reflected in the disjunctive market correction in 2000. Most of them lacked a unique value proposition. That will always be a competitive differential.

[michael hammer]

reengineering revolutionary

a business mind who wants to change the business world – now!

Michael Hammer (born 1948) is, along with James Champy, a name that's synonymous with the term "business reengineering," a fact that has won him both praise and criticism – praise from those who followed the methodology to make quantum improvements in the way that their companies do business, and damnation from the many workers laid off by companies which did not follow the methodology but merely used the buzzword to justify massive layoffs.

His bestselling book (with Champy), *Reengineering the Corporation: A Manifesto for Business Revolution* (1993, HarperBusiness), laid the groundwork for the entire reengineering movement. His fourth book, *The Agenda: What Every Business Must Do to Dominate the Decade* (Crown Publishing), was published in 2001.

Formerly a professor of computer science at MIT, he heads his own consulting firm, Hammer & Company, serves on boards of directors of several high-tech companies, and consults to the leaders of many of the world's most progressive companies. An extremely talented speaker, his public seminars are attended by thousands of people each year.

BusinessWeek named Hammer as one of the four preeminent manage-ment thinkers of the 1990s; in 1996 *Time* included him in its first list of America's 25 most influential individuals. You can learn more about Hammer at *http://www.hammerandco.com*.

In this interview, Hammer shows how emphatically he believes in the need for busi-nesses to reengineer their approach to a broad spectrum of business and opera-tional issues. Further, he hints that tomorrow would not be too soon for many companies to begin drastic change efforts. "The enemy" must be fought. Today!

Why is reengineering "revolutionary"?

For me, it's a revolution on a world scale, on the level of importance of the Industrial Revolution 150 years ago; but paradoxically, in many aspects the Reengineering Revolution is the opposite of the Industrial Revolution. Whereas the Industrial Revolution focussed on individual tasks through work specialization, the Reengineering Revolution con-centrates on the whole process, focussing on the complete work of each person.

Who are the main enemies inside the company?

They are all those afraid of change, all those who want things to remain as they are. Inside the organization, I would say there are two types of enemies. On one side, "top management," who do not really know how to be leaders and, deep down, are mere business "administrators." If they don't act like leaders, they can't achieve success. On the other side, "middle management." For these people, keeping the old system is ideal because it's the most practical thing. But I would say that if there were strong leadership from top managers, the ones in the middle would cooperate.

And what about enemies outside the organization?

Outside? Well, this may seem strange for me to say, but the most significant enemies are all of the various kinds of temporary improvements in the business environment. When the economy improves a little, when the stock market is well, everybody is tempted to relax. From one moment to the next, business leaders and executives think themselves real genies, very clever. The manager of a big bank once summarized that relaxed state of mind: "Nobody should mistake a fantastic stock market with intelligence." And I sincerely think he is right. The stock market is rising, good luck! But that doesn't mean that the company is at the right place and headed where it should. Companies have to persevere seriously in making the changes that have to be done. And the first time there is a slight improvement doesn't mean it is time to relax.

Many argue that the reengineering concept is very much talked about but few really apply it.

Looking only at the US, there are hundreds of corporations that are doing it successfully. I know of many examples of companies that have really managed to elaborate winning reengineering projects. And, in my opinion, this is one of the main factors that explain the recent success of the North American economy. While it is true and obvious that at times there are improper uses of the concept, in general terms I think that reengineering is clearly a success, and the Reengineering Revolution is, effectively, in very good shape. I even think that reengineering did a lot better than anyone ever thought it could. I am also very impressed with, and optimistic about, the capabilities of companies to facilitate their own reengineering projects.

Where has reengineering succeeded?

Reengineering developed in different ways in different industries. In the automobile business, for example, there has been a great acceptance. In the US, all the great automobile and parts factories have already started to apply the concept. The same happened with the telecommunications sector. These industries represent the first phase of reengineering. The second involved other industries like chemicals, utilities, petrol, consumer goods, and electronics.

But *only* big corporations?

Yes, the pioneers of reengineering were essentially the big corporations. But today we are already in a third stage, in which firms of smaller dimensions, such as health, banks, and insurance companies, have followed the movement. And at this moment, reengineering efforts are

In general terms I think that reengineering is clearly a success, and the Reengineering Revolution is, effectively, in very good shape

blossoming in other less predictable areas, such as retail, and even in the government.

Critics argue that such radical changes are appropriate only for businesses with financial problems. Do you agree?

That thinking belongs to the past. Five years ago maybe 80 percent of the businesses that implemented reengineering faced serious financial problems. At this moment, the percentage must have gone down to 20 percent. Today, 70 percent clearly do reengineering to prepare themselves for a different future, while the remaining 10 percent do it to attain a competitive advantage.

Today, which is the more important area of reengineering: processes or management practices?

That is an extremely important question. My answer is both. I think that there is still a very strong need in the reengineering of work processes, such as sales and product development. That is what happened recently with Kodak, to quote a case. Today there is a greater attention to management processes than some years ago. That is important because it shows that businesses understand that to change the work processes it is necessary to build other management methods.

Can reengineering be done quickly?

That is a question with several answers. The first is that the reengineering of processes depends on the size of the company concerned. The redesign of a multinational may take about two years. Some results are attained in only eight months, but the total change takes more than a year to be made. However, for easier processes it may be concluded in the period of nine months to two years on average. The reengineering of the whole organization depends on the number of processes that we intend to change at the same time. To change various aspects simultaneously is a very complex task.

But in *The Reengineering Revolution* (1995, Harvard Business School Press), you say that the reengineering effort is a five-year commitment.

Yes, but it depends on the dimension. For example, the reengineering of Delco took a period of three to five years, because it is a corporation that makes millions of dollars and operates around the world. Therefore, the effort has to be much bigger. There is not a sole answer, but one thing is for sure: in reengineering it is necessary to present results quickly. Today managers live permanently with that pressure of having to present results in the short run and to make their businesses competitive in the long run.

What's the shelf life of reengineering as a topic of management concern?

In an often-cited edition of *Fortune*, there was a box in the first pages about the loss of popularity of reengineering, which said that it is no longer a hot issue. In my opinion, it really became a less attractive business for the consultant firms but it is still a very real concern for the businesses. Reengineering is no longer a new idea, it naturally has become a part of any business. Through conversations with my clients, I notice that many are already able and willing to do it by themselves.

[charles handy]

social philosopher

a business mind with an eye on social consequences

Few "business thinkers" can lay claim to being a "social philosopher." Charles Handy (born 1932, in Ireland) began his advanced education with a classical Oxford program in "Greats" (the intellectual study of classics, history, and philosophy), reflected in his book, *Gods of Management* (1986, Oxford University Press), in which he identifies four Greek gods (Apollo, Zeus, Athena, and Dionysus) and the organizational/management styles represented by each.

After gaining real-world business experience with Shell International in London and southeast Asia, Handy entered MIT's Sloan School, where he worked with pioneers in leadership and organizational theory such as Chris Argyris, Edgar Schein, and Warren Bennis. A founder and for many years a professor at the London Business School, Handy became well known to many in the UK as the chairman of the Royal Society of Arts and for his "Thoughts for Today" on BBC Radio's *Today* program.

His influential writings examine businesses as communities, knowledge as the lifeblood of those communities, and "the new alchemists" as the magicians who have been able to overcome the inertia of traditional organizations to make great things happen – to "sow the seeds of the future." His writings range from a college textbook, *Understanding Organizations* (1976, Penguin) to boardroom classics such as *The Age of Unreason* (1989, Harvard Business School Press) and *The Age*

of Paradox (1994, Harvard Business School Press) to more unconventional busi-
ness/philosophy books such as *The New Alchemists* (2000, Trafalgar Square).
Handy was honored twice with the prestigious McKinsey Award for articles he wrote
for the *Harvard Business Review.*

In this interview, he discusses the changing corporate world and what that means
for society and for individuals. Handy looks at the marketplace and sees "elephants"
and "fleas" – and lots of change for businesses everywhere.

You define a company as a community and you say the workers are, in effect, "citizens" of the company.

If businesses no longer "own" the people they employ, it follows that
they have to have a different kind of relationship with them. That relationship is like that of a country and its citizens. Citizens have certain
rights: residence, justice, free speech, a share in the wealth of society,
and some kind of say in how it is governed. Translated into corporate
terms, a citizen's right to residence means some guarantee of employment. That doesn't mean a job for life any more, but I can envisage
employees making contracts that will last for an agreed period of time,
rather as members of the British Armed Forces bind themselves to
three- and five-year contracts for service.

How can organizations work more efficiently?

I'm not sure if we can use the term "efficiency" in the new economy, by
which I don't mean e-business and certainly not dot.coms, though of
course e-business is a factor that we can't ignore. Speed, flexibility, and
transparency of communications have had the effect of dividing the
business world into what I call "elephants" and "fleas." As opposed to
old-style corporations, fleas are small, agile, creative, unpredictable,

and above all adaptable. Examples are the growing numbers of con-
tractors, freelancers, independent consultants, and small, specialized
suppliers on which the elephants increasingly depend. What matters is
that they should deliver on time, to cost, and to specification. They are
effective rather than efficient. It's not doing things right but doing right
things that matters.

What does that mean for management?

What I think you are asking is how the flea model operates and how it
can be managed effectively. Well, look at the film business. There are no
big studios any more, just a few elephants – a director, producers, and
money men – who get an idea, assemble a team of fleas – actors and
technicians – make the film, collect the money from distributors, and
then dissolve the team. Woody Allen's film company and Steven Spielberg's Dreamworks are examples of this type of enterprise: without per-

A crucial skill will be to find where the fleas are and assemble the right team of fleas for the job

manent, money-draining investment in people and plant, such a company thrives in good times and bad.

A crucial skill will be to find where the fleas are and assemble the right team of fleas for the job. They will often be working remotely, from home or from some office of their own, so trust is a key part of the relationship. But how can we trust people we don't see and who aren't around? Communication helps, and you can hardly have too much of it. At the same time business travel is continuing to increase alongside the varieties of electronic communication. So are conferences in which leaders from all sections of business and the community can meet and share their ideas.

Has the new economy changed the way companies need to manage people?

The relationship has changed. In the old loyalty- and job security-based organization, employees were prepared to hand over the ownership of their ideas unconditionally, but that is no longer the case. They know that the assets of the organization are largely made up of what is in the heads of the people it employs. So the fleas are striking up new bargains with the elephants. We can find one sign of it in the film world. When the titles roll at the end, what we are seeing is the fleas visibly being given the credit for their contribution. That is what makes them employable in the next job that comes up. They will also expect a much greater share in the fruits of success than the arbitrary reward structure allocated to them in the old-economy organization. A reflection of that is the huge sums of money that go to the stars who bring in the audiences.

crucial

You claim that the classical organization concept will not be valid any more. What's coming?

I believe that the organization of the future will be federal. Federalism is a means of linking independent bodies in a common cause. There are already examples of this – ABB, Unilever, and Nike, to mention some examples. They operate what are in effect independent companies; Unilever doesn't even have any brands under its name. In federal companies there is a center but not a headquarters. The center does not direct or command but coordinates and operates on the basis of subsidiarity, which is that responsibility and decisions should be pushed as far out and down the organization as possible. Federal firms bring together their brains from around the world to agree strategy and aims. They do not issue edicts from the top.

How does capitalism affect society?

One effect that capitalism is having is to widen the gap between those at the top and those at the bottom. In some US companies the CEO is earning 500 times more than the lowest-paid worker. That is creating ghettos of resentment and poverty which I think capitalism will have to address because society – and hence customers – is beginning to

skill

demand it. There is a growing call for companies to behave in a socially acceptable way: look what happened to Shell in Germany over the protests of the company's policy in Nigeria. I think we are moving towards a new, more complex bottom line in which profit, environmental concern, and social responsibility will have to be in balance. Those are the forces that will shape the new society.

This requires a new mindset from corporations, but there are benefits in that for them. Take the effect of the Internet. It poses a real threat to traditional organizations. All kinds of intermediaries are disappearing from the screen as their role is called into question. How do you create value when so many goods and services are commoditized? One way is to turn to new markets or to think about markets in a new way. A case in point is Lever Hindustan. It has found a profitable Asian market for cosmetics in sachets costing a few cents and distributed through village traders, whereas its customers were unable to afford a couple of dollars for the same stuff in a bottle. The new economy needs a new, flea-like mindset. That is why big elephant companies are developing activities as venture capitalists and business incubators to keep the fleas who come up with the ideas. The new model of growth is to create business opportunities in which the fleas can flourish and develop their management skills.

Are people's lives thus becoming harder?

Yes, but they can make choices, especially the young, between freedom and commitment, time and money. That's why there's so much interest now in the idea of the work/life balance.

If balance is important, what about selfishness?

The big danger in the new relationships between people and corporations is that they lead to the creation of a very selfish society in which nobody feels any obligation toward anybody else. We are already seeing the results of this in the crime-ridden streets of prosperous European cities. I don't believe that business can flourish outside the moral order. Selfishness, or at any rate self-interest, is a natural human condition, but it ought to be what I have called "proper selfishness," a realization that pure selfishness, in which every man is out for himself, is counterproductive in that it destroys the society which makes the enjoyment of life possible.

[oren harari]

competitive strategist

a business mind always ready to "jump the curve"

Oren Harari (born 1949) is the widely read columnist whose cogent thoughts on competitive advantage have made him a popular speaker as well. He has authored or co-authored seven books. The most recent – *The Leadership Secrets of Colin Powell* (2002), *Jumping the Curve* (1994, Jossey-Bass), *Leapfrogging the Competition* (1999, Prima), and *Beep! Beep! Competing in the Age of the Roadrunner* (2000, Warner Books) – are packed with fast-reading text which reflects the man. He is a deep thinker who can quickly express a detailed opinion about what is, and is not, a strategy that will work in the marketplace.

Harari served as a senior consultant in The Tom Peters Group before founding his own firm in 1996. He is also a professor of management at the Graduate School of Business at the University of San Francisco. Whether with clients or students, Harari excels at anticipating how major external forces (such as globalization, technological advances, and shifts in consumer expectations) will impact competitive strategy.

While he has written for numerous journals, he is best known for his "Harari At Large" columns for The American Management Association. Harari was also featured on PBS/The Business Channel's documentary studying how one enterprise can "leapfrog" another. As he notes in his book on this subject: "The marketplace today is marked by upheavals that none of us could have imagined even a few years

ago. Markets are fragmenting and splintering, becoming less and less predictable. Waves of consolidation are routinely followed by waves of divestitures and restructurings. Barriers to entry in industry after industry are crumbling, and new businesses are bubbling up in market arenas that didn't exist just a few years ago."

For more information about Harari, visit his Web site at *http://www.harari.com*.

In this interview, Harari explains how business leaders can navigate such intense market upheavals and actually emerge as winners.

Every company thinks it has a strategy, yet so few seem to be operating with a true competitive advantage. Why is that?

There are several reasons. Strategy is often equated with planning, and the traditional planning process is slow, static, and reactionary. It cautiously, deliberately generates a rational roadmap based on today's realities even as explosive changes in deregulation, globalization, and technological advance continually rip up the marketplace. The planning process relies on certain premises about technology, capital markets, competitors, alliances, value chains, customer expectations, sales, cash flow, employees, and geopolitics; all these premises *may* be appropriate today but will probably be vastly different tomorrow. In free markets, new technologies are often quickly harnessed by new competitors forming new alliances in order to radically alter existing products and services and to challenge existing business models and value chains. All that screws up carefully developed plans. In short, the thick multi-year document that often emerges from the traditional process makes sense as long as the market doesn't change significantly; but since that's usually not the case, the document is often outdated and irrelevant.

A strategy, then, can be a competitive *dis*advantage?

If we're talking about a fundamental direction, a set of key priorities, a clarification of non-negotiable values, and the like, then strategy is crucial. The problems begin with the traditional planning process cited above. Further, the mountains of analysis by like-minded experts often yield "me too" strategies. That is deadly because in today's marketplace, being unique, different, special, and best-of-breed is essential for competitive success. "Me-too" strategies are not merely tepid, unexciting, and overly cautious – they make the organization indistinguishable from competitors in the minds of customers and investors. That, in turn, has serious adverse consequences for margins, customer loyalty, market "buzz," employee innovation, and investor confidence.

Another problem is that strategies are often incremental in orientation; they add features or "improve" something that already exists. For example, helping a company deliver an existing product faster and

"Me-too" strategies are not merely tepid, unexciting, and overly cautious – they make the organization indistinguishable from competitors in the minds of customers and investors

cheaper or apply better marketing and sales efforts. Incrementalism is necessary for survival, but genuine and sustained competitive advantage is about breakthrough.

Was the nature of a competitive advantage different ten years ago? Will it be different ten years hence?

Ten years ago there was more stability, predictability, and order in the marketplace. Relatively speaking, there were finite and known competitors; customers with limited choices and options; long-standing and accepted "rules of the game"; and entrenched good-old-boy networks for raising capital, distributing goods, and building sales. All of these "givens" are under assault today. It's clear that the marketplace ten years hence will be shaped exponentially by disruptive forces like e-commerce, wireless telecoms, neural networks, biotechnology, genomics, optical computing, and nanotechnology. It's also clear that the politically chaotic push towards borderless free markets will continue. The market leaders in ten years will be those who most quickly, nimbly, and imaginatively capitalize on these forces. I foresee enormous flux and vast possibilities over the next decade.

How can one feel comfortable deploying a strategy when the marketplace is operating in such unpredictable ways?

I'm not sure "comfortable" is the right, or even desirable, word any more. Strategy used to be more comfortable: done in a closed boardroom, with fellow executives and high-priced consultants, sending the grand plan for others to execute – very linear, hierarchical, rational, orderly. It's still the way things are done in many companies, but this approach is also very unrealistic. "Comfort" is precisely why so many companies get into ruts. People get comfortable – even when com-

plaining about inefficiencies and perceived inequities. They get comfortable with relationships, routines, systems, products, habits, and "what we've always done" and "how we've always done it." This "comfort zone" gets companies into trouble.

What makes for a truly competitive strategy?

I use four criteria.

- First, is the strategy *unique*? Does it reflect a new business model, break the rules, do something that's unequivocally world-class, best-of-breed, special? Is it so unique that it intrigues, excites, even dazzles customers – and investors?

- Second, is the strategy *coherent*? Does it generate clarity, commitment, and consensus among employees (and, ideally, outsiders too) as to our priorities and values?

Companies that catapult over conventional wisdom in order to carve out new value propositions or create new markets are the ones that create sustained competitive advantage

- Third, is it *deliverable*? A great idea is worthless without execution.

- And, lastly, is the strategy *ever-evolving*? Does the company have a process in place to ensure that the priorities and infrastructure we've set up to execute the strategy do not stagnate?

Who's doing strategy right?

Many companies are. Companies that catapult over conventional wisdom in order to carve out new value propositions or create new markets (think Enron, Southwest Airlines, Virgin, Sony, Siebel Systems, Dell Computer, Martha Stewart Omnimedia) are the ones that create sustained competitive advantage. This requires an ability to quickly make obsolete what doesn't work any more (no clinging to sacred cows) and quickly capitalize on fleeting opportunities (technologies, alliances, niches, service enhancements, etc.) that the marketplace offers. It also requires painstaking attention to the details of speedy execution.

And passion? Emotion?

Competitive advantage is heavily dependent on emotion: customers who are wild about a product, or feel joy about a service; investors who are thrilled; employees who are zealous and imaginative. Strategy is incorrectly approached as an analytically detached exercise, long on logic and rationality, short on emotion. Look at the companies I've mentioned (Enron, Southwest...) and you'll see that their CEOs (Jeff Skilling/Enron, Herb Kelleher/Southwest, Richard Branson/Virgin, Nobuyuki Idei/Sony, as well as Tom Siebel, Michael Dell and Martha Stewart) are all marked by a commitment to business fundamentals and fiduciary responsibility but also vividly marked by a passion and obsession verging on fanaticism. They've also demonstrated other emotions, like urgency, courage, and bullheadedness. That's why those companies have been able to achieve what conventional wisdom has said was impossible or unrealistic.

If a company has a competitive advantage, can it be "protected" any more?

Classical barriers to entry, while still relevant, are becoming less and less potent. The capacity to access global risk capital and emerging technologies coupled with enormous opportunities for niche entry, outsourcing, and global alliances means that any company, regardless of size, even in capital-intensive businesses, can now become a viable player. A company with an effective strategy proceeds "as if" there is no "protection" any more. The best strategies keep the company continually innovating, continually reinventing itself, continually making itself obsolete before the market does.

You have studied the field of competition for a long time. What are the three top lessons you have learned?

Winners do strategy on the run. Companies that are always moving quickly, always scanning the environment and horizons for opportunities, quickly/flexibly/agilely capitalizing on them, quickly generating some action plans, quickly racing to execute, and quickly redefining themselves in line with market realities (today's and tomorrow's) are those which will be the winners in the "new economy."

Intangibles are more important than tangibles. Size, mass, tangible assets, and balance sheets can be leveraged for wins; but in terms of leapfrogging the competition and creating sustained shareholder value, they are less important than factors such as knowledge, talent, imagination, speed, flexibility, responsiveness, caring, courage, and innovation.

It's gotta be fun. In the most successful companies, from fast-growing startups to established businesses like Southwest Air and Microsoft, employees say, "I'm working my butt off, but I'm having a lot of fun." Strategy can, and perhaps should, involve informality, humor, celebrations, and shenanigans at work. But more important, I define "fun" in terms of being given the tools, training, freedom, and accountability to be imaginative, develop new ideas, make changes, create something bold and exciting. That is fun. Show me a company that breathes and pulsates that sort of fun, and I'll show you a company that's probably doing some pretty interesting stuff. If strategy is not fun, if it's just a mechanical process, then it doesn't inspire employees or top management, which means it's unlikely to inspire customers and investors either.

[rosabeth moss kanter]

change master

a business mind who has keenly measured the dimensions of change

An internationally recognized business leader, award-winning author, teacher, and expert on strategy, innovation, and the management of change, Rosabeth Moss Kanter (born 1943) has delivered keynote speeches to hundreds of trade associations, civic groups, and national associations in more than 20 countries. A professor at Harvard Business School, she served as editor of the *Harvard Business Review,* and conceived and led the Business Leadership in the Social Sector (BLSS) project, involving more than 100 national leaders. Professor Kanter has received 20 honorary doctorates and, in 2001, received the Academy of Management's highest award for a "distinguished career of scholarly contributions to management."

She is the author of 15 books. These include the bestsellers *The Change Masters* (1983, Simon & Schuster), *When Giants Learn to Dance* (1989, Simon & Schuster), *World Class* (1995, Simon & Schuster), and, most recently, *Evolve! Succeeding in the Digital Culture of Tomorrow* (2001, Harvard Business School Press). She has been named one of the 100 most important women in America by the *Ladies Home Journal* and one of the 50 most powerful women in the world by *The Times* of London. She has served on the board of overseers for the Malcolm Baldridge

National Quality Award and co-chaired the Youth Service Advisory Board for Colin Powell's America's Promise organization.

A founder of the consulting firm Goodmeasure, Inc., Prof. Kanter produced "A Tale of O: On Being Different," one of the world's best-selling videos on workplace diversity. She also hosts "Rosabeth Moss Kanter on Synergies, Alliances, and New Ventures" in the Harvard Business School Video Series. For more information, see *http://www.goodmeasure.com*.

In this interview, she talks about the influences and aspirations that lie behind her work.

Is there a strand that links your work?

Every five or six years I've had a major theme and a major book. Each, I hope, has broken new ground. But always I have stressed innovation: how to create new value, how to unleash new ideas and bring them to

Culture is not fuzzy attitudes; it includes all the pieces of the organizational structure and the culture of innovation

market, how to solve complex problems, how to make organizations – and the world – better places.

One thread is that organizations have cultures and they affect the behavior and performance of people in the company. My first book, *Commitment and Community* (1972, Harvard University Press), defined a theory of organizational arrangements which promoted commitment. It was one of the first discussions of corporate culture. The corporate culture boom came a full ten years later. I am very interested in system dynamics and cultures which arise from that, the roles and norms, and how they influence people's behavior. That explains why some people succeed and others fail, some companies grow and others do not.

Culture is not fuzzy attitudes; it includes all the pieces of the organizational structure and the culture of innovation. Innovation partnerships, alliances, and global connections are also major themes in my work. They come together in the subject of culture.

Then there is the theme of change, the processes by which things happen, how we get things done. Once you understand the pattern, the dynamics of the system, you can set about changing things. How to make things change includes the necessary leadership skills, the steps in the process, and whether you have a culture which allows for change.

Another theme is empowerment. When more people are involved and making a contribution, then performance increases. Ideas and competencies too often lie buried within organizations.

Are you an idealist?

I am a very realistic idealist. They I have put forward work. They are useful and effective. We sometimes think of idealists as setting out a utopian vision, but my work is very empirically grounded. It is based on research, not on an artificial model. I believe that things can get better.

We can strive for higher degrees of excellence. We don't have to settle for grim and boring workplaces or products which aren't of the highest quality.

Do you have any sense that things are improving?

Yes, organizations have improved – though it is easy to slip. Workplaces have improved all over the world. Organizations are now faster and more diverse. Most have professionally trained managers, and more women. There is much more emphasis on leadership.

We have been going through 20 years of striving for new organizational models which move us away from machine-like bureaucracy. There is still sweatshop-type labor in which people have no chance to think, but in the global information age the mental component of every job has become bigger and more important.

New organizational models are now accepted. There is, for example, less hierarchy, more emphasis on alliances and partnerships, and encouragement of innovation. Even so, lots of companies have policies which look and sound right – like flexible working – but which don't actually happen. Managers are often not very good at motivating people or treating them well. There is a lot of lip service.

There are a lot of concepts which have been proven in practice yet are not used. Look at gain sharing for example. This is where the cost savings which result from employee ideas are shared among employees. Every organization which has used gain sharing has found that performance has improved. So, why doesn't everyone do it?

Have you got an answer?

There is still a tendency to hold onto power at the top of organizations. There are a lot of turf battles and the like. People cling to their old behavior. To some extent it is human behavior, but it is also encouraged by corporate cultures.

If organizations have been changing for 20 years, to what event or date do you look back as a turning point?

The new wave was starting in terms of practice in the late 1970s. There was a big productivity crisis in the early 1970s; global competition became a factor in the late 1970s; and then we had the first of the new consumer-oriented IT companies. The microprocessor was born in 1973 and Apple in 1977. My 1977 book, *Men and Women of the Corporation* (Basic Books), was about the old-fashioned machine bureaucracy in which people's performance was inhibited because there was no opportunity for growth or access to power.

I would date the modern corporation to around 1980 when the giant corporation first started to realize that a new type of company was beginning to emerge

At that time, my consulting company Goodmeasure got a contract with General Motors which was then working on quality-of-working-life programs and wanted to develop the diversity of its workforce. I got insights into a giant corporation trying to change. I also worked with a major computing firm which wanted to increase its productivity. It was very different, younger, more interested in new ideas. It was an alternative model.

So I would date the modern corporation to around 1980 when the giant corporation first started to realize that a new type of company was beginning to emerge.

But large corporations didn't suddenly embrace the new ways of working outlined in your 1983 book, *The Change Masters*?

No. Companies looked at *The Change Masters* and said its ideas were unrealistic. Five years later they were practicing them.

What was the next stage in this organizational process of change?

The opening of the World Wide Web in the early 1990s accelerated the process, made the new model more important, and added a few twists.

Would it be correct to see your new model as compassionate capitalism?

It is capitalism with a human face. Back in 1996, when there were newspaper headlines announcing that capitalism had won, I warned that if the business community wasn't attentive the headlines would be soon announcing that socialism was back. Now there is a huge backlash.

This was reflected in my book *World Class,* which is very much an activist's book and which looked at the need among companies, communities, and regions to create an infrastructure for collaboration.

There are strong social responsibility themes in my work. At the same time I believe that globalization can bring positive benefits if investments are made locally. I believe that government matters, public policy matters, and can effect the creation of entrepreneurial organizations.

What needs to be done to make capitalism effective and popular?

To save capitalism it needs to be inclusive and to pay attention to people at all levels. The global economy needs to work locally.

How is your take different on what is happening in the corporate world?

What distinguishes my work is that it's not flashy. It tends to be grounded. One of the reasons I continue to be based at a university – though I consult and am involved in other things – is that base in research. Some people whose ideas have become popular produce work which is based less and less on deep research. A university reminds you of the need for depth.

Who were your mentors?

I didn't really have mentors as such. As a woman in this field I was generally the first and only. I didn't have deep guidance, though people like Warren Bennis, Peter Drucker, and numerous colleagues, including my business partner and husband, Barry Stein, helped me along the way.

What would you regard as your skills?

I think I am good at synthesizing a great deal of information and seeing patterns, their significance, and defining the patterns. You have to be able to cut through the clutter and the data to say what's important.

What is the key question you ask when you go into a company?

What are you trying to accomplish – and what's standing in your way? I want to find out about goals and decisions at the corporate and individual level, what really drives people. Sometimes it's very clear. People point to missions, but sometimes these missions don't link to what's happening. Then the next question is: *What strengths do you have to help you get there?*

If you had one question for the managers of the world, what would it be?

What worries you the most – what keeps you awake at night? I always want to know about problems, trends, what's emerging, what's bothering people: what Peter Drucker calls "discontinuities." What doesn't fit?

[w. chan kim and renée mauborgne]

value innovators

two business minds who uniquely define "value innovation"

W. Chan Kim (born 1952, in Korea) and Renée Mauborgne (born 1963) are professors at INSEAD, Fontainebleau, France. Previously Professor Kim was a professor at the University of Michigan Business School where both studied.

Their work has appeared in publications worldwide. Most notably it is built on a backbone of articles which first appeared in the *Harvard Business Review*. These are "Value innovation: the strategic logic of high growth" (January–February 1997); "Fair process: managing in the knowledge economy" (July–August 1997); "Creating new market space" (January–February 1999); and "Knowing a winning business idea when you see one" (September–October 2000).

Both Kim and Mauborgne are fellows at the World Economic Forum, Davos. In all their work, they stress how "value innovation differs from traditional strategy in both the height of its ambitions and the breadth of the way it defines customers." They explained this difference at one point by stating: "Value innovation places an equal emphasis on both value and innovation. Value with no innovation stresses improv-

ing the net benefit to the customer or value creation. Innovation with no value can be too technology driven. Value innovation grounds innovation in buyer value."

More information about these business minds can be found at *http://www.insead.fr*.

In this interview Kim and Mauborgne discuss the genesis of their work and the concept of value innovation.

How do you describe your concept of value innovation?

Kim: Value innovation makes the competition irrelevant by offering a quantum leap in buyer value in existing markets and by inventing an unprecedented set of utilities to create new markets. It redefines established market boundaries. It takes a constructionist view of the market where market boundaries are formed in the minds of managers according to their beliefs and assumptions on who competes with whom. It challenges accepted and assumed market order and focusses on creating cognitive reorderings in managers' strategic thinking.

Value innovation is a strategy concept distinct from either value creation or technology innovation

Value innovation places equal emphasis on value and innovation. Value without innovation can include value creation that simply improves the buyers' existing benefits. Innovation without value can be too technology driven. Like Starbucks coffee shops, the fashion house Ralph Lauren, or Southwest Airlines, value innovation can occur without new technology. Hence, value innovation is a strategy concept distinct from either value creation or technology innovation.

How did the concept develop?

Mauborgne: The genesis of value innovation lay in the stimulation we received from European industry. Many of our examples are European. Coming to INSEAD was an inspiration for us. By being outsiders in Europe, we were able to see clearly how some companies were breaking out of the pack of competing and creating new business space. These companies had shifted from a supply-driven – outcompeting – to a demand-driven – market-creating – strategy. This helped us to realize that, at the end of the day, companies must shift the productivity frontier to a new terrain. They can only do this through value innovation, not through value improvements.

So you looked at companies going for big leaps rather than incremental embellishments?

Mauborgne: In the US, before we came to Europe, there was a group of companies, such as Home Depot, which were doing things differently. They weren't part of the establishment, they stood apart. We saw the same in Europe. There was Accor's Formule 1 hotel chain in France. Students stuck up their hands and told us about Virgin. European companies were also doing things differently. Then we started to theorize it.

We met with a lot of leaders and when they discussed industries they talked in the same way as Americans. The issues and the analysis were the same. Consistent patterns of strategic thinking could be seen the more we probed. We also saw that while these companies were innovating, they were not necessarily innovating in technology or science. They were innovating first and foremost in the value they delivered to buyers.

Kim: We found that defining companies by their national market or industry sector was not relevant. When you look across countries and companies in growing industries there is commonality. As we shared that information and the stories people told us about their national champions, our research process evolved. It was self-generating.

Mauborgne: The companies at the periphery were changing things, so we looked at what peripheral companies had in common. What could we learn from their example? Then the companies moved into the mainstream, which gave us some credibility.

We started to see peripheral companies coming to the core and creating new wealth. We tried to understand. Why? What is the strategic thinking behind it?

And what did you find?

Mauborgne: We found that there are six conventional boundaries to competition, ranging anywhere from the definition of the industry, to strategic groups to the buyer group an industry focusses on. The companies that were creating new market spaces were not bound by these traditional boundaries. Instead of focussing on competing within these well-established domains, they focussed on creating across these boundaries. Yet the strategy literature is limited by industry boundaries, such as SWOT analysis.

Creating new market space means that rules of competition – such as the five forces framework based around thinking about specific industries – become extinct when a company's objective is shifting the productivity frontier itself.

Value innovators looked at customers differently. Rather than focussing on differences between customers – which leads to ever greater segmentation and customization – they sought out commonalities, links between what customers valued.

Kim: There are generally two schools of thought on how to compete and achieve growth. First, there is the positioning school which suggests that companies need to choose an attractive industry and then position themselves within it. This takes an industry's conditions as given. It also encourages companies to allow the competition to determine the parameters of their strategic thinking. Competitiveness is based on perceived advantages over the competition.

Then there is the capabilities school, which works from the inside out. It is the resource-based view. Companies identify what they have and think of what they can do best with it.

But these two thoughts aren't enough. Despite their strengths, neither systematically addresses the strategic challenge of innovation, new demand creation and with it new business space creation. The theory and analytic tools in this domain need to be built. Value innovation and the related family of concepts we have been developing are an attempt to start to build this third school of thought.

Why can't companies just mine their existing market space?

Kim: Wealth can be created in existing market space but new market space takes companies into the future. So companies need to maintain and create market space.

Neo-classical economics assumes that one company's strategic move isn't going to change demand. But a value innovator creates demand by not playing a market share game in the existing market space. It creates new demand.

Companies can create demand?

Mauborgne: They must do so. As production exceeds demand in more industries, innovation and new business space are the top priorities. In the past, supply and demand were often in equilibrium, or demand was sometimes higher than supply. The contribution of the Japanese in the 1970s brought us greater productivity and greater competition. Now supply exceeds demand across many sectors. It is a macro-economic fact. So we need to understand how to create demand.

A value innovator creates demand by not playing a market share game in the existing market space. It creates new demand

And we can't leave this to mysterious market forces?

Kim: Traditionally we have done. Innovation in classical economics is about random choice, it happens, and so companies tend to rely on people who are very intuitive and to believe that they can't control innovation. But value innovation doesn't have to be totally random. Value innovation is the crux of strategy, not the result of one genius. There is such a thing as a brain cluster. The real challenge is to decode what individuals do.

Mauborgne: The question then is how do you create value innovation in a more systematic manner and in a manner which is sustainable? We want to show the patterns of strategic thinking, decodifying the thinking processes in a company using the research method of cognitive science. Decodifying to enable people to maximize their full potential. This requires a deep understanding on the psychology of human thinking.

Given the excuses managers routinely provide for not putting your ideas into practice, aren't you pessimistic about the possibilities of this happening?

Kim: There has been a degree of skepticism, but I haven't been to a company that didn't want to be the best. A laggard can leapfrog a leader. A settler company can shoot itself up into pioneer status. Companies can come back.

After all, most companies have more talent than they know, but they don't take advantage of it. Innovation can be indigenous. The assumption is that we require more diggers, but it should be about where to dig.

Aren't we too busy digging to actually think about how innovation occurs?

Mauborgne: That is the problem. Many CEOs don't have time to figure out why their company was successful. It was successful implicitly. Star players go and a company doesn't know what made it successful and then the performance starts to fall. Companies increasingly want to institutionalize what made them successful so that their success can be more sustainable.

Kim: There is a certain level of resistance to rethinking what you're doing and have been doing. People want to stick to the status quo. Their resistance is not to value innovation. There are no analytical insights, no formulated strategic vision to make things happen. There are no methodologies, how-tos or path-making suggestions.

Isn't this like having to go somewhere new without a map? CEOs must shake things up, but there is no formula for doing so.

Mauborgne: CEOs have seen funds move to companies with new ideas. They feel capital market pressure. As exchanges come together in Europe, the capital in one company can move from Siemens to Vivendi or Pirelli. Shifts in capital mean there is a perpetual need to innovate. A recent survey of business executives shown in *The Wall Street Journal Europe* put innovation as the number one strategic priority of companies in the upcoming years.

So CEOs must take the lead?

Kim: We envisage process-based theory rather than it being CEO-based. The CEO doesn't have to give a speech about a vision for analytics to connect to the brains of the people. It is difficult for CEOs to embrace a theory and then to spread it to top managers. Usually theories aren't analytically oriented. The trouble is, theory needs analytics. In our work we try to create a balance between ideas and analytics. When we deal with our MBA students we see the young, the old, the innovative, and the uninnovative, but the theories have to work for all. You need ideas which stimulate their creativity while supported with analytics and how-tos.

Mauborgne: Another issue is that more and more companies are nervous about fads, and CEOs are concerned about following highfalutin aims. Increasingly CEOs need the support of analytics. This is especially true in innovation which the economics discipline has traditionally treated as an exogenous factor largely beyond the control of firms. The New Growth Theory of economics spearheaded by Paul Romer, however, challenged that assumption and started to prove otherwise. Our aim is to try to help CEOs here by building theories and analytics to help

More and more companies are nervous about fads, and CEOs are concerned about following highfalutin aims

reduce the risks and increase the probabilities of successful new business space creation.

Is there an ideal organizational structure with which to achieve value innovation and uncover new market space?

Mauborgne: We don't think there is an ideal structure for value innovation *per se*. Whether centralized or decentralized, functionally oriented or not, there is no solution through structure. But there is a process of interaction. Each structure has its own merits and problems. We see how process can overcome weaknesses of structure to capitalize on structure. This is the theory of fair process. The key to making value innovation happen is implementation of fair process.

What do you mean by fair process?

Kim: Basically, if managers think that a company's processes are fair, they are more likely to trust the company and be committed to it. Essentially, fair process comes down to what we call the 3Es – engagement, explanation, and expectation clarity. Engaging people in the decisions that affect them, explaining the basis of final decisions and why decisions need to be taken to begin with, and setting clear expectations of the rules of the game in moving forward and what is expected of people. The result is voluntary cooperation, active idea sharing, and intellectual and emotional persuasion.

When you go into a company what is the question you ask?

Mauborgne: Our question is simple: *what is it that makes companies exciting, confident, and strong?* Innovation is about the life of a company and

we are having fun looking inside of companies – both leaders and lag-
gards – to understand the way forward.

If you're presented with a new business idea what's the first question you ask of it?

Kim and Mauborgne: Where and how will this new business idea change
our lives? Is there any value innovation potential here?

What distinguishes a lasting management idea from a fad?

Kim and Mauborgne: There are three criteria:
1 Is there a strong causal link to performance?
2 Is there strong theoretical reasoning and/or, equally important,
   common-sense reasoning that explains this causal performance link?
3 Are there analytic tools and systematic processes or paths that allow
   companies to act on this insight and institutionalize it without
   undue complexity?

A fourth criterion, though not a necessity, is: Does an idea have the
power to intellectually and emotionally engage an organization and
make the people better for having been a part of it?

What question would you like to ask the managers of the world?

Kim and Mauborgne: What have you been doing to make a difference to
our society in general, and to you and your people in the organization
in particular?

[philip kotler]

marketing doyen

a business mind who has defined "marketing" for the modern age

Philip Kotler (born 1931) has led the marketing debate for more than 30 years. Along the way he has coined phrases such as "mega marketing," "demarketing," "social marketing," "place marketing," and "segmentation, targeting, and positioning." His 25 books include the definitive textbook on the subject: *Marketing Management: Analysis, Planning, Implementation and Control* (1999, Prentice Hall).

Kotler has done more than probably anyone else to cement marketing's reputation as a serious business discipline. He regards marketing as the driver of company strategy and the essence of business. "Good companies will meet needs; great companies will create markets," he writes. "Market leadership is gained by envisioning new products, services, lifestyles, and ways to raise living standards. There is a vast difference between companies that offer me-too products and those that create new product and service values not even imagined by the marketplace. Ultimately, marketing at its best is about value creation and raising the world's living standards." He has repeatedly said: "Marketing is not the art of finding clever ways to dispose of what you make. It is the art of creating superior customer value." In spite of such lofty claims, the attraction of Kotler's work is the balance between accessibility and authority.

Kotler's lengthy academic career – based at Northwestern University in Chicago – has charted the shift from "transaction-oriented" marketing to "customer relationship marketing." For more information, see *http://www.kotlermarketing.com*.

In this interview, he talks about the genesis of his career and state of the art of marketing.

What ignited your interest in marketing?

My training is in economics. I studied under Milton Friedman at the University of Chicago, and then for my PhD under Paul Samuelson at MIT. Both are Nobel prize winners but with very different economic perspectives. Friedman believed in unfettered markets and Samuelson in macroeconomic policy. I thought that I would work at the level of micro economics, how things actually worked in the marketplace. I went back to the early literature – people like Edward Robinson of Harvard and Joan Robinson at Cambridge – who in the 1930s worked on the theory of monopolistic competition and saw that demand was influenced by sales force and advertising as well as price. But mainstream economists preferred to work with price theory since it was more tractable. In 1960, I was invited to join a year-long Ford Foundation Harvard program to train business school professors in higher mathematics. This involved 60 fine scholars and I spent most of my time with the marketing group and found the marketing problems fascinating. I examined current marketing textbooks and was disappointed to find them heavily descriptive and lacking analysis and a decision orientation.

My first book, *Marketing Management* (1967, Prentice Hall), introduced to the field a decision framework, one dealing with such questions as how to optimally set sales force size, advertising, price, distribution channels, and so on. This led to my second book, *Marketing Decision*

Making: A Model Building Approach (1970), which analyzed the same problems in terms of advanced economic theory and mathematics. In subsequent books, I brought marketing theory into new domains: marketing for nonprofit organizations (museums, performing arts, hospitals, colleges, etc.), marketing social causes and ideas, marketing places (cities, regions, and nations), and marketing celebrities.

Were there any particular mentors in this?

I have always respected Ted Levitt at Harvard for his tremendous insights. And I learned a great deal from John Howard and Jagdish Sheth at Columbia who produced a very analytical view of consumer behavior.

A chief marketing officer can bring a lot of market realism to senior management deliberations

Isn't there still a shortage of people with marketing backgrounds at the very top of companies?

There are many companies now run by people who've come up through marketing. But corporate boards tend to focus on financial issues, especially in multi-divisional companies. They tend to think that a marketing person can't say much of value because marketing challenges vary from division to division. That's a mistake. A chief marketing officer can bring a lot of market realism to senior management deliberations.

What other misconceptions are there?

Too many CEOs see all marketing expenditure as expense, rather than recognizing a chunk of it as investment, namely that it builds soft assets. In the agricultural economy, owning land was the most important thing. Then, in the industrial economy, it was owning a factory. In the information age, intangible assets are decisive. More senior managers now realize that value lies in softer assets not recorded on the balance sheet – the company's brand equity, the capabilities of employees, the size and loyalty of the customer base, the loyalty of distributors, and the company's intellectual capital. We are seeing more companies go virtual, preferred to own brands and relationships rather than factories.

Another misconception is that a company makes the most money by paying the employees, the suppliers, and the distributors the least. This is zero-sum thinking. The new view is that the companies experiencing the most sustained levels of profit and growth are those which are generous to their stakeholders and see business as a team sport.

What annoys you most about people's perceptions of marketing?

I am bothered because the public only sees the tip of the marketing ice-berg – the irritating commercials, the junk mail, and phone calls. This results from mass marketing where the company hasn't carefully defined who might need their product or service. Companies really don't want to spend money reaching people who won't buy. They are increasingly trying to target better to those who are real prospects and to stop annoying the others.

And the public rarely sees the great care that major companies give to their close customers. Marketing isn't only hunting; it is also gardening. It is not only meeting the current needs of your customers but envisioning new ways to make them better off.

Part of the problem is that companies set up a factory and must keep it running. So some of marketing consists of hunting for new customers. When marketing works, it not only makes money and meets needs, it also produces and sustains jobs.

Isn't marketing so all-embracing now that it has become invasive?

Today's hot subject is customer relationship marketing (CRM, also called one-to-one marketing, database marketing, etc.). The idea is that when a company knows more about each customer, it can serve each better by customizing its product, service, and messages. It won't pester those who aren't in the market. However, there is growing concern about what companies know about each of us. The public is pushing the government to limit what companies can find out about individuals. As privacy concerns grow, CRM will lose some of its potential effectiveness. Today responsible companies are asking customers for

permission to reach them with news and offers, rather than blanketing everyone with uninvited offers. That's the purpose of the "unsubscribe" choice at the bottom of e-mails.

What do you think, therefore, about the anti-capitalist protestors who feel that brands are too powerful?

The anti-capitalist protestors are a mixed group: environmentalists who see global businesses as ruining the environment, unionists who see their jobs taken away by foreign workers, animal rights people, and many who want rich countries to cancel the debts of poor countries. Capitalism is in trouble and it hasn't delivered on its potential. We are waiting for a more humane version of capitalism that worries about the poor and about the obscene salaries of the rich. Capitalism will lay the seeds of its own destruction if it doesn't find new markets; the rich can only consume so much output. I am sympathetic with the ideas of

Capitalism will lay the seeds of its own destruction if it doesn't find new markets; the rich can only consume so much output

people like Hernando de Soto (the Peruvian economist) who wants to monetize the property of poor people so they can use it to get loans and who wants to see more generous micro-finance lending to entrepreneurial women in poor countries.

What is the most important question you ask when you visit a company?

Who are your target customers and which needs of theirs are you trying to satisfy? The great Sears department store used to answer: everyone and every need. Today this would be suicide.

The second question is: Have you put together a truly superior offering compared with your competitors? If not, what are you going to do about it? Today it is hard to see a difference between United Airlines and American Airlines, Hertz and Avis, Pepsi Cola and Coca-Cola.

Which companies do you regard as benchmarks?

The marketing geniuses are companies that deliver a new set of values in their respective industries, companies such as Dell, Southwest Airlines, Virgin Airlines, Charles Schwab, IKEA, Saturn, Sony, GE, and Harley Davidson. And these companies remain leaders because they continuously introduce new sets of value into their respective industries.

Most companies get too routinized, asking for the same budget each year, allocating it in the same way. It takes a Jack Welch to warn them: "Change or die."

How do you tell the difference between a fad and a great management idea?

It's hard to predict in advance which ideas will be fads. People will always hitchhike on a new idea and push it to the limit. I take a Darwinian view where the good ideas will survive because they have functional value, and the poor ones will wither away. In my field, segmentation, targetting, and positioning has stood the test of time. Today we are elaborating such ideas as customer equity and brand equity and I believe they are sound and will be long lasting. CRM and customer lifetime value are also sound, as is integrated marketing communications.

My regret is that there is not enough debate in marketing over different ideas. An exception is whether products and brands pass through fairly predictable life cycles, with P&G saying no brand has to die and others saying that brand life cycles do occur.

Another debate concerns how brands are built. The traditional idea is that brands are built by advertising. I would counter by saying that advertising produces awareness, possibly interest, maybe trial. But brands are basically built by product performance in relation to the brand promise. I would go further and say that more companies would be smarter to cut their advertising budget and put the same money into better service performance and innovation.

How do you split your time?

I am a restless researcher trying to apply marketing thinking beyond products and services. I divide my time among researching/writing, teaching, public speaking, and consulting. I view myself as a thinker, coming up with new ideas, concepts and models. I get my kicks from developing new perspectives and recognizing market trends in

advance. I always think of the future not as something that will happen later but as something that has already happened somewhere and the signs are present.

What effect has the advent of the new economy and the Internet had on your thinking and on marketing?

I am doing research on the new economy which is really about a company's ability to manage its future through information. I am working with colleagues on a concept of "holistic marketing" where a company combines the informational power of enterprise resource planning, supply chain management, and customer relationship management to leverage greater success in the marketplace. Central to holistic marketing are the marketing uses of the Internet, the company intranet, and various company extranets to create a competitive edge in the company's drive toward profitable growth.

I expect that the price transparency of the Internet will put great pressure on prices

My current research is taking two directions. One is to develop real-time marketing "information dashboards" where managers can check on a daily basis on sales, prices, and costs in different geographical and segment markets. This will enable them to discern latent growth opportunities and also detect and respond to problems emerging in the field.

The other research direction is to create "planning dashboards," whereby brand managers have available in the computer everything they need to know in developing a marketing plan. They can find out how to test a marketing concept, what kind of sales promotion might work best in a given situation, how to judge the effectiveness of an ad, and so on. It would represent a marketing encyclopedia of "best marketing practices" in the computer.

I believe that the Internet will fundamentally change business and marketing practice. I expect that the price transparency of the Internet will put great pressure on prices. I expect the emergence of business-to-business Web sites will reduce the number of sales people involved in routine sales work. I expect to see companies increasingly differentiating their services to different tiers of customers according to customer lifetime value. In preparing my 11th edition of *Marketing Management*, I hope to show how customers, suppliers, distributors, competitors, and marketplaces will change in the Information Age. And the change will even be more profound with m-marketing (mobile marketing), where the cellular phone or wireless Palm becomes our source of e-mail, the Internet, chatting, and even a payment system replacing credit cards.

[john kotter]

leadership's leader

a business mind finely tuned to how leadership drives change

John P. Kotter (born 1947) has been called "the best speaker in the world on the topics of leadership and change." A graduate of MIT and Harvard, he has been on the Harvard Business School faculty since 1972 and in 1980 was among the youngest faculty members ever given tenure and a full professorship.

A prolific writer, seven of his business books have won awards or honors, and more than a half dozen have become business bestsellers. These include *Leading Change* (1996, Harvard Business School Press), *Corporate Culture and Performance* (1992, Free Press), and *A Force for Change* (1990, Free Press).

His biography of Konosuke Matsushita, *Matsushita Leadership* (1997, Free Press), won a *Financial Times* Global Business Book Award. Other awards include an Exxon Award for Innovation in Graduate Business School Curriculum Design; a Johnson, Smith & Knisely Award for New Perspectives in Business Leadership; and an annual McKinsey Award for best *Harvard Business Review* article.

Kotter is dedicated to finding the formula for effective leadership. He considers it critical to any business or organization. As he says in his Preface to *Leading Change*, leadership is the critical ingredient for driving change. "A purely managerial mindset," he argues, "inevitably fails, regardless of the quality of people involved."

In this interview, he provides insights into his career development and focusses on the essentials of leadership as he sees them after years of studying the subject with intensive academic research.

Is there a logical development in your career?

The simple logic is that I am a pure field guy. I hang around talking to people. I talk to managers. I sit and watch them. I snoop around, listen to their problems. My work is developed by looking out of the window at what's going on. It is about seeing patterns. If I'm good at anything it's pattern analysis and thinking through the implications of those patterns. So, as the world has evolved, my work has evolved, though personal interest also shapes what I look at.

My field is managerial behavior. My doctoral thesis was a managerial behavior study. Then I did work on managerial careers – that was part of understanding managerial behavior and the history of it all. For my book *General Managers* (1986, Macmillan) I hung around with staff. As I watched what was happening during the 1980s the whole notion of leadership cropped up more and more. What I was saying was that what managers call leadership – a piece of their work – was growing in importance.

My first book on leadership, *The Leadership Factor* (Free Press) came out in 1988, then I figured out that differentiating between management and leadership was important – 90 percent of people doing management stuff thought that it was leadership. The system didn't support leadership, so I did a culture study. Then I looked at economical and environmental changes, discontinuities. I saw how they were affecting the careers of Harvard Business School graduates. From there I increasingly understood that leadership and change were closely related. I looked at a whole bunch of situations involving transformations.

The next step was to do an in-depth study of a fascinating leader, so I did a biography of Konosuke Matsushita, founder of the eponymous Japanese corporation, whom no one, in the United States at least, knew anything about. It was another cut at the whole thing. Some big insights came out of that which I'm still working through.

Let's talk more about change. Is there a "most significant" guiding force in initiating a change effort?

There are many forces that will impact the success of a change effort. For example, change is easier to implement in small corporations, and deregulated environments allow for faster changes in a shorter time. But at the outset of a change initiative, the most important guiding force is competitive urgency. Change is hard work that takes serious, long-term commitment. Urgency is a key motivator that allows change agents to stay focussed and serious about what needs to be done.

Urgency is a key motivator that allows change agents to stay focussed and serious about what needs to be done

Urgency needs to be the driver because more than anything else, more than any other organizational issue, it inspires.

Isn't it obvious that urgency would be the prime motivator in most change efforts?

Not at all. Organizations change for all sorts of uninspiring reasons: others are doing it, stock prices are relatively flat, it seems like a good idea, a new chief executive wants to stamp his or her mark on the company, the latest bestseller is telling everyone that they have to change immediately. It's going to be very hard to motivate a senior change team, not to mention the majority of employees, around such causes.

Failing to establish a sense of urgency is one of the key mistakes made by change leaders. In Leading Change you discuss seven additional steps in successful change efforts.

That's right. Beyond establishing a sense of urgency, organizations need to create a powerful, guiding coalition; develop vision and strategy; communicate the change vision; empower broad-based action; celebrate short-term wins; continuously reinvigorate the initiative with new projects and participants; and anchor the change in the corporate culture.

What does this "guiding coalition" look like?

The guiding coalition needs to have four characteristics. First, it needs to have position power. The group needs to consist of a combination of individuals who, if left out of the process, are in positions to block progress. Second, expertise. The group needs a variety of skills, perspectives, experiences, and so forth relative to the project. Third, cred-

ibility. When the group announces initiatives, will its members have reputations that get the ideas taken seriously? And fourth, leadership. The group needs to be composed of proven leaders. And remember, in all of this the guiding coalition should not be assumed to be composed exclusively of managers. Leadership is found throughout the organization, and it's leadership you want – not management.

Who needs to be avoided when building this team?

Individuals with large egos – and those I call "snakes." The bigger the ego, the less space there is for anyone else to think and work. And snakes are individuals who destroy trust. They spread rumors, talk about other group members behind their backs, nod yes in meetings but condemn project ideas as unworkable or short-sighted when talking with colleagues. Trust is critical in successful change efforts, and these two sorts of individuals put trust in jeopardy.

"Communication" seems to crop up in most discussions of organizational effectiveness, and certainly in discussions of effective change. What do you mean when you use the term?

Effectively communicating the change vision is critical to success. This should seem obvious, yet for some reason, executives tend to stop communicating during change, when in actuality they should be communicating more than ever. Effective change communication is both verbal and nonverbal. It includes simplicity, communicating via different types of forums and over various channels, leading by example – which is very important – and two-way communication. Change is stressful for everyone. This is the worst possible time for executives to close themselves off from contact with employees. And this is particularly important if short-term sacrifices are necessary, including firing people.

How important is "continuously reinvigorating" the initiative?

It's critical, but sometimes difficult to accomplish. Major change is usually a long-term commitment that is often filled with sacrifices. Those sacrifices might include layoffs, plant closings, pay reductions, and significant changes in long-standing corporate policies, values, and ways of doing business. You're asking people to cope with high stress and high risk, in the hope that the key decision makers really understand and know what they're doing. Reinvigorating the initiative continually motivates people by reminding them of where the organization is going and why. The most obvious ways to reinvigorate a change effort are by bringing new people into the process who will convey fresh ideas and energy; or to offer up new, motivating projects and challenges. But reinvigorating a change initiative can also be very simple – as easy as celebrating short-term wins.

Major change is usually a long-term commitment that is often filled with sacrifices

What is the value of a short-term win in a long-term initiative?

Short-term wins show progress in the direction set by the organization itself; demonstrate that the change ideas are working; increase morale among workers who may be slipping into cynicism or suffering from the fatigue that change and stress engender; give you a chance to throw a party and say thanks; and, they build momentum. Short-term wins are a reason for people to stay with the program.

What if things like celebrating small wins and open communication are contrary to the existing corporate culture? Should the culture, then, be the first thing to change?

In any major organizational change, the culture is the last thing to change. Organizational cultures are deeply ingrained value systems, not susceptible to simple rhetorical appeals. Cultures change over time, when new behaviors are demonstrated, successes are chalked up, and when new people and ideas are on board.

In your experience, do your ideas about change translate well internationally?

I have studied hundreds of change efforts around the world and have not found any important difference between the corporations I have observed on both sides of the Atlantic that have tried, over the past ten years, to become stronger competitors. When competitive urgency is the motivator, then the forces that impact successful change initiatives appear pretty universal.

What makes a great management idea?

Great ideas capture something important about reality which people haven't seen but once you see it, it leads to an action and helps people do better things. It's important that they're actionable: people change from doing X to doing Y. $E=MC^2$ is a phenomenal example of capturing a truth in nature in an efficient way with huge actionable implications. Managerial ideas need to capture something of human nature or organizations that are not just a function of what's happening this year or last. Fads tend to be not quite Barnum & Bailey but Hula-Hoops. People come up with a term they can sell at the time. It is a question of fashion. If it is not based on a fundamental truth, it comes and then goes.

[edward lawler]

management master

a business mind who is a master of management across the board

Edward E. Lawler III (born 1938) is the author of 34 books and more than 300 articles which range from studies on compensation to employee participation to the right organizational structure for the 21st century. He is the Distinguished Professor of Business at the Marshall School of Business at the University of Southern California and the founder and director of USC's Center for Effective Organizations.

Lawler is the recipient of the highest research awards given by the University of Southern California, The Human Resource Planning Society, the Society for Industrial and Organizational Psychology, the Academy of Management, the American Society for Training and Development, and WorldatWork. *Workforce* magazine identified him as one of 25 visionaries who, between 1922 and 1997, shaped today's workplace.

His latest book, *Corporate Boards: New Strategies for Adding Value at the Top* (2001, John Wiley) (co-authored with Jay Conger and David Finegold), examines the roles corporate boards should play within the 21st-century corporation and the behaviors that can make boards successful. Lawler has written extensively on employee reward programs and employee motivation. His book *Rewarding Excellence: Pay Strategies for the New Economy* (2000, Jossey-Bass) is a classic in the field. For additional background, log onto *http://www.EdwardLawler.com*.

In this interview, Lawler considers the vital, though often overlooked, role of boards of directors in the corporate world.

Your latest book says that "corporate boards are in the spotlight." Why is this and why did you choose to study them?

There's a growing focus on boards, mainly because people are seeing the critical role they play not only inside a company but in society as a whole. The CEO/Center for Effective Organizations, which I helped to start 22 years ago, has now grown to the point where we have more than 50 companies involved in a number of projects. I have interacted with board members over the years, and I have sensed that the role of a board has been changing. I wanted to know more about that. Jay Conger and David Finegold were not only key to the research for the book, they were also true partners in our assessment of where boards today are – and where they need to be.

You have also noted boards in the future will be different because of the Internet. Isn't that an odd intersection?

Just a couple of years ago, we polled the corporations involved in the CEO to see how they wanted to receive communications from us. Then, half said by Internet, half said by paper. Today, it's 100 percent Internet. But it's more than simple communication. My co-author, David Finegold (thanks, in part, to support from Korn/Ferry, the international recruitment firm), has been really investigating this question and will have some breakthrough findings in a couple of months. For now, we can see that board members (who are generally not of the digital generation) are occasionally using the Internet for virtual meetings. They are starting to use the power of online communication to get updates

on what's happening inside the companies they're governing – from corporate culture issues to real-time financial readouts. And, of course, they are getting official company info almost instantaneously.

In general, is it hard to get the "right" kinds of people to serve on boards? Are we still living in an age where the CEO's friends make up his or her board?

Having only friends of the company chairman on the board is becoming less and less true. That said, the typical board is not as diverse or as independent as it should be. This is not just a US issue – no country has cracked this problem fully, although some of the legislation in Europe that mandates worker representation on boards is noteworthy.

A board is a group, perhaps in some cases a team

To this point, you talk about "new governance forms." What would be the *one* structural thing that would most change the character of a traditional board of directors?

Look at all the ruckus over recent World Trade Organization meetings, both in Seattle and Quebec. What's the core issue there? It's readdressing the question of who governs corporations and who corporations should serve. This goes beyond management and leadership. Governance studies boards in an almost political sense – whether they are looking out only for the shareholders of the company or whether they care about *all* the stakeholders. To be sure, if employee interests, supplier interests, perhaps even customer interests were all represented on boards, companies would behave much differently.

If employee interests, supplier interests, perhaps even customer interests were all represented on boards, companies would behave much differently

So we should have more women and minorities on boards?

Membership is not just a gender or race issue. While board membership today hovers around 10 percent female (and much less for Asians, Hispanics, and Blacks), it's *how* board members govern that's at issue here. Women on boards today often see their role as the same as that of their male counterparts. We need board members who see their role differently – regardless of gender, race, or ethnicity.

Quickly, for you: what's a "high-performance" board?

Potentially, boards have three resources to use: power, information, and knowledge. When these three resources are present and effectively directed at, first, handling emergencies, second, making sure an effective strategy is in place, and third, truly influencing the decisions of the chief executive officer (and who succeeds the CEO), then we can say that the board is acting in a high-performance way.

But there's another key point that should be stressed. A board is a group, perhaps in some cases a team. What Jay, David, and I have tried to do is look at boards through the lens of group and organizational effectiveness. Boards need to be assessed by the same conditions and behaviors that lead groups to be effective.

And what is group effectiveness?

Here's what we said in our book: "Group effectiveness is the product not of simply one element but rather a combination of behaviors and practices converging to create an effective unit. The research on organizational effectiveness clearly shows that in order for groups to be effective decision makers, they need *information, knowledge, power, rewards* that motivate, and *opportunities* to perform their duties as a board." I still believe these are the keys to effectiveness, to becoming a "high-performance" board. What boards need to do is to think of themselves as a group which can use these tools to become better and thus to guide their respective companies in more enlightened ways.

What's next for you?

Our center issues a tri-annual survey of management practices among Fortune 1000 companies, and the next one is due shortly. What I'm most fascinated about is the increasing issue of knowledge and how it's managed inside corporations. Of course, this is a natural tangent to the impact of the Internet, which is affecting everyone inside companies, and not just boards. Seeing organizational change over the decades, as I have, it's easy to become jaded. But I'm not. This is an exciting time to be inside a company. And it's an exciting time to be studying how they're managed.

[david maister]

management professional

a business mind who has been called "the professional's professional"

David Maister (born 1947, in the UK) is a different kind of management guru. While most business researchers and business books have focussed on industrial companies, Maister has spent his career studying and advising the professional services firm, that is, the accounting, legal, consulting, executive search, and real estate industries – firms which have nothing to sell but their people and their accumulated knowledge and skills.

As an academic in the early 1980s, he committed to writing a monthly article for *The American Lawyer* for three years. Those articles, plus others he published elsewhere, drew attention to him and his work. His first book, *Managing The Professional Service Firm* (1993, Free Press), was a compilation of his articles. The books that followed have been translated into a variety of languages. His latest book, *Practice What You Preach* (2001, Free Press), is based on his findings from a survey of more than 100 businesses across the world.

Fast Company said of him: "David Maister is the man the country's top advisers go to for advice." Maister holds degrees from the University of Birmingham, the London School of Economics, and the Harvard Business School, where he was a professor for seven years. For more information on his ideas and background, visit *http://www.davidmaister.com*.

In this interview, Maister outlines what he learned from studying the correlation between employee attitudes and financial performance in 139 professional offices.

When you first visit a company, what is the most important question you ask?

What are the non-negotiable, minimum standards of behavior in this company? A company, I believe, is not defined by its aspirations but by the operational standards it is willing to enforce.

You have now studied the management practices of hundreds of "professionals." What did you learn overall?

Of all things that professional firms do, managing people is consistently rated lowest on the list. However, the most financially successful offices consistently do better at all aspects of managing people.

Curiously, differences in performance are predominantly due to character and skills of individual managers, not the systems of the firm

A kind of "science" is emerging in the field of professionalism. I'm now certain that, without knowing firm size, line of business, client mix or country of operation – just knowing the employees' answers to nine specific questions – I can predict more than 50 percent of the differences in financial performance. Curiously, differences in performance are predominantly due to character and skills of individual managers, not the systems of the firm. More than that, performance of successful managers is mostly due to their character and their belief systems, not individual tactics.

Is there a connection here to making a profit?

What I have proved – and I stand by the word "proof" – is a strict sequence for making money, which goes like this. If you want to make money you've got to serve the marketplace to incredibly high standards. To do that you have to energize, excite, and enthuse your people. To do this, you've *got* to have skilled managers. That is the "big bang" of management. If you can do that, you will make more money. The bit I've got proof of is only with a marketing communications business. Therefore I have to be careful. But I'm bold enough to say that this finding is applicable not just to professional services firms but to business in general.

This *does* sound somewhat like Management 101...

In some ways it is! Success is not about systems, processes, or management fads; it comes down to a very simple question: Do you have the managers in place who know how to manage? Do you have managers who are creators of passion, drive, and ambition in others? If you've got managers who know how to do that in others, then you will create the nuclear chain reaction. But managers who can do that turn out to be a *very* scarce resource.

So if companies want to boost their performance…

To improve performance, companies should focus not on their quarterly financial targets but on motivating staff to provide excellent service. You make more money by doing the basics very well. Someone in one of the case studies in my last book said: "Chasing money is not what makes you money." That's very true. Nothing in what I'm advocating is saying that money is not the goal – that's not the message. What I'm saying is that if you're interested in money, then the best way to achieve that is not by focussing on the money but by getting excellent at something that people will reward you for. That applies not just to high-end professional services, but to McDonald's. McDonald's success is based on uncompromising standards.

You've talked about standards and performance. How about relationships, another key area you've researched? Aren't most business relationships fairly up front?

Most business relationships are satisfactory, but real "trusted adviser" relationships are more scarce. Perhaps a test of the need is the reaction of many people to even thinking about this topic. They think that even talking about earning trust is "New Age" or "touchy-feely." They would prefer either to remain in the logical realm ("I'll earn my client's confidence by the brilliance of my ideas") or to remain intuitive ("I don't need to think about this, I'll just do the right thing when it happens").

But business isn't just logical, it's emotional and personal, and not all of us have trained instincts to do and say the right thing, in the right way, at the right time. One of the most common business processes today is a renewed effort to do cross-selling and key account management, that is, build relationships with major customers. Businesses are

focussing on it because, to date, they have done an imperfect job in this area.

Then something like "trust" can be managed?

There are concrete things you can do to earn trust in business, and many, many things you can do to lose it. So, yes, it can be "managed" if you're willing to be self-aware about what you do and what you say when dealing with other people. Trust is an essential ingredient in all relationships, business and personal, and it's possible to be thoughtful about it and not just intuitive. In our personal lives, when we are trying to build a relationship with another person, we try consciously to be sensitive, supportive, and understanding. We think actively about ways to show we care about the other person and use language that shows we're trying hard to be on their side and take their feelings into account. The exact same thing applies in building relationships with clients, colleagues, and subordinates.

But you do admit that trust is complex, even ultra complex?

Absolutely. Someone can trust your competence and reliability but have severe reservations about your motives – whether you will treat them fairly, live up to your promises, and look after them. They may think you're too focussed on technical issues and not on the larger problem. They may think your self-orientation is too high. The act of hiring anyone (whether it's for a legal, accounting, medical, property, or consulting issue) requires you to hand over your affairs to a stranger and trust that they will look after you responsibly. It's not just about "Can they do it?" It's a very complex, emotional process. But that argues for trying to understand its components, not for giving up all thought about it.

What distinguishes a lasting management idea from a fad?

The most important distinction to make is between a business idea and a management idea. Business ideas are rooted in logical, rational, intellectual analysis. Management, by contrast, is not about logic. It's about the interpersonal, social, and emotional skills of managers who have to deal with human beings as clients, employees, or colleagues. Thus, no idea can last unless it reflects a keen understanding of human behavior. If the idea is purely intellectual, it's likely to be a fad. And the tragedy of business education around the world is that too many managers are trained in business, not in management!

To what extent do leaders succeed or fail based on who they pick to advise them?

It depends upon how people use advisers, and many do it badly. Some seek out "an expert" and place their affairs in that expert's hands, rely-

Business ideas are rooted in logical, rational, intellectual analysis. Management, by contrast, is not about logic

ing on the expert's judgment and technical expertise. That's unwise. In my view, what leaders (and all of us) need is someone who will help us solve our own problems ("be an adviser") and not just provide answers. We need someone who will help us understand our options, give us an education on those options, provide a recommendation based on their experience, and then help us reason through to our own conclusion. That's what we mean by being an adviser, and it takes a completely distinct set of skills in addition to knowing your field. Too many busy leaders provide a hostage to fortune by hiring experts and not skilled advisers. They are taking big risks in so doing.

Ditto for leaders in other fields besides business?

None of this is restricted to the commercial sector. In fact, there are many people inside organizations of all kinds who are professional advisers even though they do not charge fees for their services. Human resource directors, marketing directors, engineers – all organizations are stocked with people whose job it is to give advice, and they are faced with exactly the same issues as those of us on the "outside." How do I win influence? How do I get people to accept my judgment? How do I get permission to try something new? In summary, how do I get people to trust me?

One senses that, in your own career, you've been burned a time or two by a bad relationship.

Haven't we all? But it wasn't the unethical, fundamentally untrustworthy person who caused me to feel burned. It was an otherwise well-meaning person who lost my trust and confidence by neglecting silly things. The lawyer who won't return phone calls when I'm dying to find out what happened. The interior decorator who won't accept responsibility for missed deliveries. I know problems occur, but can't you just keep me informed and play straight with me? The information technology consultant who just won't listen to what I want, and keeps telling me what he thinks I should want. This isn't about ethics: most people's intentions are good, but their skills and behaviors are often pathetic and annoying.

How does one keep from becoming so cynical about people's motives that no relationship seems safe, reliable, trustworthy?

Make clear, right at the start of a relationship with any provider or adviser, exactly how you like to be treated, and how you want to work together. We tend to assume (eternal optimists that we are) that *this* time it will be different. This new public relations counselor will be attentive, this ad agency will respect us and involve us in the decision making, this engineer will explain things in plain English. But we rarely ask for it up front, and we should. We should ask new suppliers to describe not only how they will approach the work but, specifically, how they work with their clients.

The good news is that, by and large, the troublesome problem is not motives but skills and behaviors. No one ever teaches us how to build and maintain a relationship, and we could all improve a lot, very quickly, by beginning to think about it.

What question would you like to ask managers around the world?

What would it take to get managers to focus on the long term? We know that business endeavors that last a long time usually have a management team that resists short-term temptations; this is true even in public companies. To survive, companies need a long-term focus, yet most managers succumb to short-term pressures. So, again, what would it take to get managers to focus on the long term?

[henry mintzberg]

practical radical

a business mind determined to know how managers *really* work

For nearly 30 years, Henry Mintzberg (born 1939, in Canada) has been a thorn in the side of traditional management education. While most academicians have focussed on how business should work, Mintzberg has concentrated on how managers *really* work. His first book, *The Nature of Managerial Work* (Harper & Row), was published in 1973 after being rejected by 15 publishers, and it has become a classic in the field.

What was radical 30 years ago is today coming into fashion. Mintzberg has held longstanding appointments at McGill University and INSEAD, where he focussed on practical management; now, traditional MBA programs around the world are starting to adapt some of the radical ideas and methods of the International Masters in Practicing Management (IMPM) program created by Mintzberg with Jonathan Gosling of the Lancaster University Management School in the UK. While traditional MBA programs stress learning about business, the IMPM program helps students learn how to manage – recognizing that students have as much to learn from each other as from the faculty.

Among the many awards bestowed on Mintzberg throughout his career are the Officer of the Order of Canada, the Distinguished Scholar Award from The Academy of Management, and a host of honorary degrees from universities around the world.

Always ready with a different perspective on the work of management, his most recent books include *Strategy Safari: A Guided Tour Through the Wilds of Strategic Management* (1998, Simon & Schuster) and *Why I Hate Flying: Tales for the Tormented Traveler* (2000, Texere). To learn more about Mintzberg, visit *http://www.henrymintzberg.com*.

In this interview, Mintzberg focusses on his iconoclastic views on strategy and other key management subjects.

You have been critical of formulaic, analysis-driven strategic planning. Why?

Because analysis-driven strategic planning is little more than elaborating and operationalizing the strategies that companies already have. That's not strategic thinking.

Why does the method fail?

Because it is predicated on three fatal pitfalls. First is the assumption that discontinuities can be predicated. They can't – at least they can't with any real accuracy. Forecasting techniques are limited by the fact that they tend to assume that the future will resemble the past. There isn't much that can be more fatal to an organization than that assumption.

The second pitfall?

Planners are detached from the reality of the organization. Planners have traditionally been obsessed with gathering hard data on their industry, markets, and competitors. Soft data – networks of contacts, talking with customers, suppliers, and employees, using intuition and using the grapevine – have all but been ignored. To gain real understanding of an organization's competitive situation, soft data needs to be dynamically integrated into the strategy process. While hard data may inform the intellect, it is largely soft data that generate wisdom. They may be difficult to "analyze," but they are indispensable for synthesis, which is the key to strategy making.

And the third?

The assumption that strategy making can be formalized. The left side of the brain has dominated strategy formulation with its emphasis on logic and analysis. Alternatives which do not fit into the predetermined structure are ignored. The right side of the brain needs to become part of the process with its emphasis on intuition and creativity. Planning by its very nature defines and preserves categories. Creativity by its very

Planning by its very nature defines and preserves categories. Creativity by its very nature creates categories or rearranges established ones

nature creates categories or rearranges established ones. This is why strategic planning can neither provide creativity nor deal with it when it emerges by other means. The real challenge in crafting strategy lies in detecting the subtle discontinuities that may undermine a business in the future. And for that there is no technique, no program, just a sharp mind in touch with the situation.

If you're right, then the "golden age" of strategic planning and perhaps reengineering is over. If so, where is management headed?

I don't like to play that game. Nobody can predict. The world heads in different directions all the time – who knows which one will dominate? It is absolutely wrong to tell managers what is going to happen next.

Fair enough. How about MBA programs? As a long-standing critic, your comments have had important impacts in America and Europe. What is wrong with MBA programs?

MBA programs train the wrong people in the wrong ways for the wrong reasons. The MBAs are B-programs, business based – not A-programs, about administration (meaning management). People think they are being trained as managers. What kind of managers? They learn to talk, not to listen. Management education should be based on experience. Managers cannot be made *in vitro*.

Would you care to predict which of the many influential programs might dominate during the first part of the new century?

I hope ours [the International Masters Program in Management which Mintzberg helped launch] do, but I still don't care to predict.

In your examinations of managerial work, you found that managers did not do what they liked to think they do.

That's right. I found that instead of spending time contemplating the long term, which is what managers often are assumed to be doing, managers were slaves to the moment, moving from task to task with every move dogged by another diversion, another call. The median time spent on any one issue was a mere nine minutes.

So, if managers aren't continuously pondering the future, what are their roles?

Managers must perform at three broad levels: informational, people, and action – all three both inside and outside their units. That is one *demanding* job.

Your book *Why I Hate Flying* essentially condenses all of these thoughts about strategy and the practice of management.

It is a spoof on management looking at the management practices of airlines and airports from my experience. "Welcome aboard ladies and gentlemen, this is your author scribbling," is the opening. At the beginning of each chapter there's a piece on how the airline and airport experience relates to management. For example, it looks at how change management – "change always comes first" is one of the lines – converts passengers from cattle into sardines; customer service means constantly interrupting passengers as they try to sleep; and customer loyalty means rewarding people so they fly on other airlines.

Who would you pick as the most influential management thinker?

Peter Drucker had a lot of ideas, he was undoubtedly a great influence. But I would also name Herbert Simon. He is not very much talked about among the management community, but he had a deep influence on the issue of how the decisions of the manager are made. He changed the way of looking at organizations. In an historic perspective, I would name Frederick Taylor as the most influential. We still practice Taylorism on a large scale.

A lot of contemporary thinkers are writing about the Internet and the new economy.

I do not think that one should exaggerate. What the Internet is doing is to deepen a direction that has been developing in the past 50 years in the sense of a greater fluidity of the manager's job. I do not think that that is new. What is happening is that it is being accelerated. The more recent e-business puts additional pressure in the same sense.

If you go into a company, what is the most important question you ask?

I would ask no questions before I see, on the ground, with my own eyes, what is going on in the place – what it looks like, how it seems to work, who its people are, etc. I have done this often in consulting, and it has proved invaluable.

What questions would you like to ask the managers of the world?

Are you making the world a better place? Do the people who report to you think so?

[ian mitroff]

organizational whisperer

a business mind who believes organizations need the "whole person"

Ian Mitroff (born 1938) is often cited as "the father" of the discipline of crisis management. Befitting that title, he is the president of Comprehensive Crisis Management as well as the founder and past director of the University of Southern California's Center for Crisis Management. Yet, as Mitroff would tell you himself, this is only a part of his interests and background.

Mitroff has written 22 books, which range from crisis management to spirituality. One of his early books, *The Unbounded Mind* (1993, OUP), certainly reflects the scope of its author. "I suspect that I have a different definition of management from most academics and practitioners," Mitroff admits. "For me, management is the creation of ethical means to achieve ethical ends."

Mitroff's most popular books are *The Essential Guide to Managing Corporate Crises* (1996, Oxford University Press), *Managing Crises Before They Happen* (2000, Amacom), *A Spiritual Audit of Corporate America* (1999, Jossey-Bass), and *Smart Thinking for Crazy Times* (1998, Berrett Koehler). In all the books that Mitroff authors or co-authors, one reality emerges quickly: Mitroff is both an engineer and a philosopher – his training and reading in both fields make his writing style (and scope) distinctive. He is also a professor at the University of Southern California. In addition to his advanced degrees, he holds an honorary doctorate from Stockholm University

in recognition of his extensive book writing, as well as more than 300 published articles. For more information about Mitroff, log onto *http://www.compcrisis.com*.

In this interview, Mitroff not only talks about the founding of crisis management but also about how a new "whole person" point of view can open up potential in any business. What the world needs, says Mitroff, is more "organizational whisperers."

Some managers feel that every day is a crisis. For you, what is the threshold of a *real* crisis?

A "real crisis" is any event that has the potential to destroy the organization, result in significant deaths, or wreak extreme financial havoc. Obviously, these are management calls. But that is the "real job" of management.

You note that crises are inevitable: that even the best-managed organization can confront one. Why is that? Why can't crises be "pre-managed"?

Even with the best of preparations, one does not have complete control over everything. Also, the "environment" keeps inventing new types of crises that we haven't thought about or considered. Nonetheless, the main point is that those organizations that are crisis-prepared recover substantially faster even if they cannot prevent everything.

A lot of top managers want to hide from the press when bad news afflicts their business. Is that smart?

It's dumb! Whether one likes them or not, the media are everywhere. Besides, if you avoid the press, that will only make the crisis worse.

From the companies in which you have worked, how many execs are truly getting straight talk from their employees on conditions in the workplace?

The vast majority are stunned because they are not getting straight talk. In most organizations, the messengers of bad news are "killed." But this means that managers don't get early warning signals of potential crises, the most important bit of prior information they could receive.

Why don't organizations work better?

I'm really starting to distill my thinking on that question. I've been doing it by studying the general field of "whisperers" – such as horse whisperers, dog whisperers, baby whisperers. When you really study people actually doing this kind of work, you learn that they succeed because first they recognize the whole animal or person, and second they are really keen observers of the behaviors and language of their object of attention. I'm now starting to do that with organizations.

I'm finding that, especially in management studies and businesses, people are often too quick to promote the rational over the emotional

And you're finding…

I'm finding that, especially in management studies and businesses, people are often too quick to promote the rational over the emotional. They're too quick to elevate the cognitive realm over the spiritual realm. People slot others (and they allow themselves to be slotted) much too easily. This isn't something that starts in B-schools – my research indicates that people often come into a business school class already self-divided into either a rational or emotional point of view.

For example?

Oh, say, the finance student who, deep down, really wants to work with customers or do non-financial activities, but he's self-categorized into a "finance guy" and the B-school mentality (and the business world mindset) chains him to that perception. So we have silos forming early in one's life, refortified in college, then sealed shut in the real world. It's tragic. Social shaping is real. But the world could be much, much different.

And how would you change it?

We do not allow people to integrate their thoughts *and* their emotions. We act as if thinking and emotions can be strictly separated from one another, and far too many people buy into this dumb idea! Until we learn how to talk about, deal with, and integrate into the day-to-day running of organizations what really matters to people, organizations will continue to self-destruct. We need to make some major inroads into the spiritual side of people and organizations. We need new ways to think about people and organizations, and we need new ways to measure input, output, and overall performance.

How would you ever start to do something like that?

I'm not saying it's easy, and I'm sure not saying I have all the answers. But I would start by smashing the disciplines which drive academe and which are often used to structure organizations. My PhD is in engineering and the philosophy of social science. I have never believed in disciplines. The creation of disciplines was the worst thing that ever happened to knowledge. It created artificial distinctions between fields of knowledge. The disciplines do not matter. All that matters is to think and read and study widely. Everything interacts with, and is a part of, everything else. Disciplines are mentally suffocating.

This actually ties back to your advice on managing crises, doesn't it? You note that managers should think outside the box but that execs would be wise to think *far* outside the box. Say more.

A crisis challenges all of the conventional assumptions one is making about one's business, organization, and stakeholders. That's why only those who can think unconventionally can be a step ahead. But the point can be raised to a larger context. All managers, in all disciplines, would do well to start reading people like William James and John Dewey, classic writers who had lots to say about management but have never been credited for their insights. And, today, Ken Wilber is doing much the same thing: he is a brilliant, integrative writer.

Are you thus optimistic or pessimistic about the future of management and organizations?

There's a wonderful *New Yorker* cartoon I saw once. It was a fictional baseball scoreboard with the "Realists" playing against the "Idealists." In each inning of the game, the Realists were clobbering the Idealists –

but the final score had the Idealists winning by 1–0. Sure, on any given day we can feel crunched, overwhelmed, and depressed. But taking a spiritual view, it does not pay to be cynical. That's why the notion of hope is at the center of spirituality. It can shape the future in ways that doomsday thinking simply can't. We have proven that organizations can change. If we continue to study new fields of knowledge, such as spirituality, then we can change organizations in new ways – better ways. There's every reason to be optimistic.

[geoffrey moore]

chasm guide

a business mind who is defining the age of the Internet

Geoffrey Moore (born 1946) is the founder and chairman of The Chasm Group, a California-based consultancy focussing on market development and business strategy. Though he is now a major management writer, Moore actually has roots in other professions. He started as a professor of English literature, focussing on the Medieval and Renaissance periods. He switched to business in order to move his family to California, closer to relatives. From there, he spent ten years in sales and marketing with software companies, 15 years in consulting (ten with his own firm, The Chasm Group, in San Mateo), and the past four years he has spent half his time as a venture capitalist with Mohr Davidow Ventures of Menlo Park.

Moore's first book, *Crossing the Chasm* (1991, Harper), looked at how innovative companies had to cross a chasm in order to reach the lucrative mainstream market. The sequel, *Inside the Tornado* (1995, Harper), described how these companies can capitalize on the hypergrowth possibilities once they cross the chasm. His latest book, *Living on the Fault Line* (2000, Harper), addresses the question of how management of a public company needs to address shareholder value in the age of the Internet. More about him can be found at *http://www.chasmgroup.com*.

In this interview, Moore defines the challenge facing old-thinking leaders struggling to become successful in the age of the Internet.

Your most recent book talks about "shareholder value in the age of the Internet." All the e-stocks seem to be falling right now. Are you worried?

The age of the Internet should not be confused with e-stocks or dot.coms. Every company needs to incorporate the Internet into its strategy, and how it does so will impact its stock price. The key point is that the Internet fosters a new economy in which the winners will be those who leverage partnering and outsourcing more innovatively and more aggressively than ever before.

To be sure, the Internet is not going away – and it does seem to be affecting every enterprise. You talk about "plate tectonics." Why that analogy?

The "fault line" metaphor refers to disruptive changes in business models that destabilize the established power positions of incumbent market leaders and open up new competition for leadership and its rewards. Classically incumbents lag in this competition, given their legacy position to protect. The analogy I use in the book is intended to help executives understand the dynamics of this situation in a way that lets them act effectively to increase, not decrease, their shareholder value going forward.

At one point, you state: "Miss the wave, and there is no recovery." That's heavy! Do you see some business leaders drifting out to sea, or even drowning?

I have never been accused of understatement. The key notion here is that as a new technology wave displaces a former paradigm, there simply is no future unless you can catch the new wave. Think of Olivetti, Novell, Kodak, Xerox, AT&T (or any other switch-based telephone network company). All these companies have drifted out to sea, and all have thrown at least one highly competent CEO overboard.

You do a great job of talking about the evolutionary stages of growth for a company, yet you also acknowledge that a lot of companies will have to excel at all phases of the life cycle almost at once – no matter how chaotic that may seem. Can chaos thus be helpful?

Let's be clear. I hate chaos. I hate chaos cheerleading. But where chaos accurately describes the forces at work, then management needs to have at minimum a coping strategy, ideally a strategy that actually leverages the chaos. In the case of a company with multiple offers in multiple phases of the life cycle, the key coping strategy is to segregate business processes as much as possible (separate go-to-market channels, for example, separate manufacturing, separate cost structures, etc.). By contrast, a start-up looking at this situation will attack this company because it takes so much energy to keep these various threads separate and functioning that they may likely miss or misread a competitive threat.

You talk about many problems and challenges, yet you always come across as relentlessly upbeat. You even close your book by saying: "There has never been a time when there was a greater opportunity for wealth creation." Is this born optimism or have you learned it?

I may have been born with an overdose of endorphins. That said, consider that I live in a country that has never been directly touched by war and has the highest standard of living in the history of the planet, and at a time when idea wonks like myself actually get attention. How bad

can it be? As for wealth creation opportunity, there has never been more capital more broadly available worldwide for funding innovation, nor a better understanding of how that capital might be put to effective use. That said, of course we will screw things up along the path. That is the human way.

You also talk, just a bit, about courage. Why *that* quality as the very end of your book?

My experience as a consultant is that my clients mostly need only a little help to get where they know what to do (often, indeed, they have known it all along). The challenge is to get it done, and in fault line situations, this means taking on phalanxes of taboos all arrayed with spears pointing outward at you. In particular, whenever a leader must transition from one paradigm to another, there is an inevitable "nasty bit" that simply must be powered through. During this period everyone

There has never been more capital more broadly available worldwide for funding innovation, nor a better understanding of how that capital might be put to effective use

looks like an idiot, stock price tanks, and shareholders demand that heads roll. It takes courage to look this straight in the eye and say, sorry, we are headed into the nasty bit, and I am leading the charge.

You seem to pull from many disciplines to make your points: science and psychology are melded nicely with business examples and concepts. One senses you are always widely reading, listening, thinking – is that your approach? Do you recommend it for others?

I am an inveterate synthesist. If you choose this path, virtually anything you read becomes material to integrate; and so, yes, for other synthesizers, I would recommend eclectic reading choices. The key here is to get enough raw material for metaphors and analogies – a storehouse of concrete pattern representations – so that when you see a new pattern you can describe it crisply and with punch.

What's next for you?

I am working on making *Living on the Fault Line* come true. With the downturn in the economy, executives are more concerned than ever about managing for shareholder value, and their attention has turned toward the core/context distinction in chapter one and the effort to outsource as much of their context as possible to focus a greater percentage of their time, talent, and management attention on core. The challenge here is in managing a mission-critical business process when part or all of it is being conducted by an outsourcing party.

[kenichi ohmae]

provocative globalist

a business mind who sees the world through the portal of Japan

Dr Kenichi Ohmae (born 1943, in Japan) is the world-renowned expert at explaining Japan to the world and one of the few Japanese who knows how to theorize and articulate ideas in the "American thought leader" mode. After completing his PhD in nuclear engineering at MIT, Ohmae joined McKinsey & Company, where he spent 23 years and co-founded its strategic management practice. Ohmae left McKinsey to stand for the governorship of Tokyo in 1995.

He is the founder and managing director of Ohmae & Associates, JASDICK (a software development house), EveryD.com Home (an Internet platform for living rooms), and Business Breakthrough (an interactive satellite network for business). Ohmae is also the dean of two private schools in Tokyo: Isshinjuku, which studies public policy, and Attacker's Advantage, which studies entrepreneurship. He is also the chancellor's professor of public policy at the UCLA School of Public and Social Research.

His latest book, *The Invisible Continent: Four Strategic Imperatives of the New Economy* (2000, HarperBusiness), examines hot industries such as e-commerce, banking, and telecommunications, distinguishing between the old-world "titans" such as IBM, GM, and CBS, and the new world "Godzillas" like AOL, Dell, Cisco, and Microsoft. He discusses four basic forces and how a dramatic and volatile battleground is forming between companies and the countries that try to regulate them. For more information about Ohmae, his Japanese-language site may help at *http://www.kohmae.com*.

In this interview, Ohmae exhibits the thinking pattern of someone whose view of the world is shaped by his Japanese roots – and vice versa.

Is there a way to accurately characterize a "Japanese approach" to strategic thinking?

Japanese businesses tend not to have large strategic planning staffs. Instead they often have a single, naturally talented strategist with an idiosyncratic mode of thinking in which company, customers, and competition merge in a dynamic interaction out of which a comprehensive set of objectives and plans for action eventually crystallize. Forget simplistic Western myths about Japanese management. There is much more to it than company songs and lifetime employment.

Company, customers, and competition?

These three key players collectively constitute the "strategic triangle." Seen in the context of the strategic triangle, the job of the strategist is to achieve superior performance, relative to competition, in the key factors for success of the business. At the same time, the strategist must be sure that his strategy properly matches the strengths of the corporation with the needs of a clearly defined market. Positive matching of the needs and objectives of the two parties involved is required for a lasting, good relationship; without it, the corporation's long-term viability may be at stake.

Is the Japanese strategic process largely rational, in the Western sense?

The Japanese approach to strategic thinking is basically creative, intuitive, nonlinear, and so seen by most Westerners as irrational. Phenomena and events in the real world do not always fit a linear model. Hence the most reliable means of dissecting a situation into its constituent parts and reassembling them in the desired pattern is not a step-by-step methodology, such as systems analysis. True strategic thinking thus contrasts sharply with the conventional mechanical systems approach based on linear thinking, or even using strategic framework, which some scholars have developed.

Given this approach, how might Japanese management define effective business strategy?

Not all that differently than Western managers. An effective business strategy is one by which a company can gain significant ground on its

The Japanese approach to strategic thinking is basically creative, intuitive, nonlinear, and so seen by most Westerners as irrational

competitors at an acceptable cost to itself. This can be achieved in four ways: by focussing on the key factors for success, by building on relative superiority, through pursuing aggressive initiatives, and through utilizing strategic degrees of freedom. By this I mean focussing on innovation in areas which are untouched by competitors. So we might say that the outcome or objective is the same from East to West, but getting there is quite different, in that Japanese entrepreneurs use a holistic and intuitive approach at the beginning, as opposed to statistics and surveys often used in large Western corporations.

Now more than ever, strategists have to think globally. How do we best understand "global strategy"?

The essence of any business strategy, global or regional, lies in offering better value to customers than the competition does, in the most cost-effective and sustainable way. On a global scale strategists have to understand and believe that thousands of competitors from every corner of the world are able to serve customers well. To develop effective strategy, we as leaders have to understand what's happening in the rest of the world and reshape our organizations to respond accordingly. Our ability to comprehend the commonalities across the borders is equally important to our ability to develop the feel for different needs of consumers in each region. No leader can hope to guide an enterprise into the future without understanding the commercial, political, and social impact of the global economy.

Most organizations have little experience here to guide them.

Without experience as a guide, organizations will have to rely on their ability to learn and grow. The most important trait is the corporate center's eyes to see and ears to listen. However, in reality, the center

tends to become a Mount Olympus. We have to learn to share, sort, and synthesize information, rather than simply direct the work of others. We have to rethink our basic approach to decision making, risk taking, and organizational strategy. And we have to create meaning and uphold values in flatter, more disciplined enterprises. In fact, we may have to forget the past in order to create the future.

You've written for some time about the "strategic triad" – the United States, Japan and the Pacific, and Europe. Are these regions what you mean by your term "regional economies"?

No. They are different concepts. What you referred to are the gigantic "economic blocs." What we observe today is the emergence of smaller regions, with an average size of 3–10 million people, that interact with the rest of the world, with the global economy. For example, look at the rise of "global" cities in China and India, such as Dalian and Bangalore,

We have to learn to share, sort, and synthesize information, rather than simply direct the work of others

respectively. This emergence is the result of what I call the 4Is, criss-crossing the traditional national borders – investment, information, industry, and individuals. With the Internet and satellites, this trend is irreversible.

So your message of "triad power" continues to be valid?

Yes. When I created the term, I was interested in understanding what the great corporations were doing in relation to globalization. I verified that they were forming strategic alliances in the direction of some key markets around the world. What moved me was the story of how the great businesses were realigning themselves, particularly in regard to Japan, the United States, and Europe, that I called the triad group. None of those big companies could attain that positioning by itself. That's why I used the concept "strategic alliance." At that time you'd be hard pressed to find 50 such alliances; today they are commonplace. You see them in every sector: pharmaceuticals, airlines, telecommunications, banking, machinery, chemicals, and consumer electronics.

So, what exactly is a "regional state"?

For me, the region-state is an autonomous and optimal economic unit to interact with the global economy, with a population from a few million, to a maximum of 20 million. It is a space that interacts with the rest of the world, accelerating the flow of the aforementioned 4Is with the global economy. Examples are all around. Look at the triangle of Singapore, Johor, and Riau; consider the technology-based relationship between Ireland and the US; or on a much larger scale, look at India. India is transforming itself into an electronic zone, with private satellite connections to Singapore, for example, that allow it to overcome the problems of the Indian telecommunications systems. These con-

nections, together with the abundance of engineers, are attracting the multinationals. Another case is New Zealand, where the reinvention of government combined with deregulation allowed it to connect to the global economy. I would also add Finland and Denmark as more recent examples.

Do these cases you quote have much in common?

They cross at three points. First, the connection to the nets, to the Internet and other similar webs. Second, the persistent restructuring of the economy of those countries in the past 15 years. Third, the fact that they speak English, and that they speak it well. This competence is vital today, not only because it is the language of business but also because it is the language of the World Wide Web. Countries like Singapore and Malaysia are adding value to their economies because they've adopted a business language that allows them access to a worldwide customer base. China may be an exception to this rule in terms of language, but its regions are amazingly free for the global capital to come in and produce wealth. In many ways, it is as though they have "ten Taiwans" on the coastal regions. Chinese region-states are much like the states in the US, and compete fiercely with other regions. That is why places like Dalian, Shenzheng, Shanghai, and Suzhou are flourishing.

Clearly, "region-state" is an important concept in strategic planning. How did it come to you?

In a very simple way. I discovered it because I go out of Japan frequently, as much as 25 times a year. As I am a good observer, I've been observing the global business for 25 years. I saw this phenomenon grow and now it is absolutely real. What I have found is that in cases where governmental power is overly centralized, you don't see these region-states grow; but where there is a balance between centralized power and autonomy, as in the case of Germany and the US, region-states flourish. A constitutional balance of power allows autonomous regions to find their own strength, discover their potential. I don't get tired of quoting a case that I think is remarkable and that happened in America: Las Vegas. Las Vegas is literally an island floating on the ocean of the American desert. It started by being a global point of the game industry. However, today it is not only gaming, it is a global center of conferences and entertainment. It is an example of that American flexibility and autonomy, which allowed an industry to go to the desert and make a profit. Orlando would be the same case, growing in a marshland, to have 40 million visitors a year and more than 2.5 million residents.

You put a high premium on personal observation.

As you know, most companies do most of their "planning" based on the reading of documents and statistics about the world. But I tell you, certain locations cannot be known and certainly cannot be understood in the absence of personal experience. Certain regions in countries such as China, India, Vietnam, Myanmar, Brazil, and Argentina – places often discussed for the strength of their labor force – have to be experienced. Companies need their own people there, to develop the "feel" for what is happening there, to know things first hand. Journalists are not a good alternative as antennae for your own business development. Documents and written words are too far removed from the real lives, politics, customs, and histories and sense of people.

[richard pascale]

edge thinker

a business mind who explores the edges of management to come

Richard Pascale (born 1938) first came to the attention of a large audience with the advent of the "Seven-S" framework, one of the most renowned and debated management tools of the 1980s. From Pascale's perspective the Seven-S model presented a way to compare US and Japanese management. Pascale and his co-author, Anthony Athos, concluded that the Japanese succeeded largely because of the attention they gave to the "soft S" factors – style, shared values, skills, and staff. In contrast, the West remained preoccupied with the "hard S" components: strategy, structure, and systems. These conclusions formed the bedrock of *The Art of Japanese Management* (1981, Penguin), one of the first business bestsellers.

Pascale was a member of the faculty at Stanford's Graduate School of Business for 20 years. He has since worked as an independent consultant and as an associate fellow of Oxford University. He is also the author of *Managing on the Edge* (1990, Viking) and co-author of *Surfing the Edge of Chaos* (with Mark Millemann and Linda Gioja, 2000, Crown). In addition to the Seven-S framework, Pascale's work is significant for a number of reasons. He was among the first researchers to provide original insights into Japanese approaches to business and management. He and Athos explored the importance of corporate vision. In addition, Pascale has explored the related areas of corporate mortality and corporate transformation. More recently, he has used the term "agility" to describe the combination of skills and thinking required of the organizations of the future and has explored the links between complexity theory, living organisms, and modern organizations. For more information, go to *http://www.surfingchaos.com*.

In this interview, Pascale reviews his career and explores how the laws of nature can be applied to the business world.

You are an educator, writer, researcher, and consultant. How do you split your time?

When I was finishing my MBA at Harvard, people were frantic for the perfect job. I found it difficult to enter into the spirit of that and was troubled by the entire process. I had an inspiration and realized what I would really like to do is spend a quarter of my life teaching, a quarter consulting to earn money and test out the relevance of the theories I would be teaching, a quarter writing (which is something I enjoy – if you put your ideas down on paper you quickly discover what you're full of), and finally a quarter of my life on holiday. I have managed to achieve that since the late 1960s, even when I was at Stanford. As I have become older, I have focussed more on large organizations and their challenges. I would describe my life as backing away from what doesn't work to a more attractive alternative.

What were the origins of your first book, *The Art of Japanese Management*?

I was consulting with the National Commission on Productivity, a board of industry and union leaders. Though I had been in Japan with the US Navy, I assumed that the reason we couldn't learn from Japan

was because the culture was so different. But then I thought I could study Japanese companies in the US – they did enough differently to encourage me to challenge my basic assumptions. I didn't define myself as a Japan scholar, but I was interested in making Western organizations more productive and in helping huge organizations change. For me, Japan was a new lens on how best to operate. The idea of vision statements, for example, came out of that. The Japanese thought that it was obvious. At that time in the West it was not politically correct for an organization to have a vision. For a company to have a position on something bigger than its results was seen as dangerously quasi-religious. The concept of shared values in the Seven-S model was not an easy sell at the time. Now it is accepted.

Then there was a long hiatus until *Managing on the Edge* was published in 1990. What happened?

When we finished *The Art of Japanese Management,* there was pressure to produce another book. I wrote a three-page outline on what I thought

In most companies, because of turf wars, egos, and the like, we are relatively inept in dealing with contention

the next issue would be. I had observed the vulnerability of the companies designated as excellent throughout Tom Peters' and Robert Waterman's *In Search of Excellence* (1982, Harper & Row). Because they were so coherent internally they were ill equipped to deal with a radical shift in the environment. I had stumbled on a law of cybernetics which says that variety in organizations shows up as contention. In most companies, because of turf wars, egos, and the like, we are relatively inept in dealing with contention. I found that contention and contradiction were seen as mismanagement. I thought I could write the book in six months, but all the data and interviews I had didn't help on what I wanted to write about. I had to go back to the start. In the end, I think, *Managing On The Edge* is a bit turgid.

In the book you celebrated Honda as the best managed company in the world. Is this still true?

I will duck that a little as I don't know the company as well now. But Honda could have been an Apple, a company with design but without the level of technical innovation necessary. Honda has kept at the frontier of engineering and design while being responsive to customers and dealing with pretty aggressive rivals.

Managing on the Edge features an attack on the managerial enthusiasm for faddish ideas. What prompted this?

The invisible assumption of management is the focus on doing. People are selected because they get things done. As long as people's radar is tuned into doing, you have no place to get hold of the underlying issues. While doing is variable, being is constant. The being of people and organizations is hard to move. The superficiality of management fads has always perplexed me. While American audiences are much

more superficial and looking for the quick fix, Europeans have a greater willingness to sit, listen, think, and read. The level of intellectual inquiry is generally not robust enough to cope with the complexity of our problems.

Is this changing?

Yes, I think that the proliferation of fads is coming to an end. Beginning in the 1980s most CEOs had the latest business books displayed on their bookshelves. It was as if the people who looked after the plants also stocked and replenished the bookshelves with the latest fad-based bestseller. Talking to audiences at that time, three-quarters had typically gone through ten fads. They were jaded and cynical. Clearly, some ideas have merit. Total quality management (TQM) is a profound management philosophy, but it was applied piecemeal, and the end result was business as usual. Now, senior executives have limited interest in the next big idea. There is a sense that the ideas are all the same and that it's capricious to screw around with an organization and then shift to the next thing six months later.

But the books keep emerging.

Yes, but it offends me to read a book that should have been an article. People have a hard enough time getting through their reading in the time they have available. Ideas need to be expressed in a few words; they can be just as useful and influential. It also bothers me when something is a recast old idea that has just been repackaged. Alternatively, it is true that some of these ideas haven't been internalized. Sometimes old ideas need regeneration and restating. Usually, however, recycled ideas encounter the same problems. How do you determine whether something is a fad or a good idea? There is no simple way. You can disturb but not predict a living system. If you introduce something like performance pay, it will have, at some stage, unforeseen effects. That doesn't mean the idea is wrong. Often a faddy idea will use clever terms and have the appearance of being a silver bullet, such as reengineering.

What motivates you to write books?

When I write a book, I write to reinvent myself; it is not about marketing or being famous. I talk about an idea for three or four years. A lot of that is in classrooms, so I get to explore the nooks and crannies of the ideas. They begin to get stale. Then it is time to ask what's missing in my own understanding of why organizations don't change. I cast around because I've got to stay fresh. That's one of the things about executives: I don't know how managers do it – day in, day out, with a week or two weeks' vacation every year. How do they stay fresh?

How did you become interested in the field of complexity and living systems?

I found that incremental change was not enough. The traditional models of how to govern organizations didn't do what was necessary. Then I began working with the CSC consulting firm on the subject of organizational change. Linda Gioja – then with CSC and one of my co-authors on *Surfing the Edge of Chaos* – suggested that there was stuff on systems and complexity which would be relevant. I was very skeptical but signed up to go to the Santa Fe Institute to a business network meeting. Their speaker couldn't make it, and they asked whether I could speak. The only thing I could think of talking about was the irrelevance of their ideas to business. They thought this sounded like fun and afterwards asked me to become a visiting scholar so that if I had a different view at least I would know what I was talking about. I got to know Brian Arthur, Murray Gell-Mann, and Stuart Kaufmann.

And you became convinced?

Yes. It took a while, but I slowly realized that organizations are living things. It is just that we have a strong mindset about organizations being mechanical. Most executives have a very mechanistic view of change.

Do you think, therefore, that the explosion of knowledge in the life sciences will have impact on the way we work?

There are great wealth-generating opportunities which will affect industries of all kinds. Our understanding of life is going to change the way we work. Historically, major breakthroughs in the sciences have preceded revisions of the language of management. At the moment, the language of management remains that inherited from Isaac Newton. As life sciences emerge, the language of management will change. Already

Surfing the edge of chaos is the hard part. It is frightening, something to be avoided, but it is an edge, not an abyss

you hear references to the DNA of organizations which assumes organizations to be living things.

Isn't the hard part converting these metaphors into reality?

The living organization is reality. The real metaphor is the mechanistic view of organizations. The four principles which are the cornerstones of the life sciences really do apply to companies. First, equilibrium is a precursor to death. When a living system is in a state of equilibrium, it is less responsive to changes occurring around it. This places it at maximum risk. Yet it takes courage to disturb this equilibrium. Organizations and individuals don't want to take a winning formula and turn it on its head.

Second, in the face of heat, or when galvanized by a compelling opportunity, living things move toward the edge of chaos. This condition evokes higher levels of mutation and experimentation, with the result that fresh solutions are more likely to be found. Surfing the edge of chaos is the hard part. It is frightening, something to be avoided, but it is an edge, not an abyss. Third, once this excitation takes place, the components of living systems self-organize, and new forms and repertoires emerge from the turmoil. This property of life is called self-organization and emergence.

Finally, living systems cannot be directed along a linear path. Unforeseen consequences are inevitable. The challenge is to learn how to disturb them in a manner that approximates the desired outcome and then course-correct as the outcome unfolds.

How did companies react when you first approached them with these ideas?

Actually, of the companies featured in *Surfing the Edge of Chaos,* three or four were already exploring the concepts of complexity and the living organization before I was. They were no strangers to it. The trouble faced by some was that they had listened to people and thought complexity was a very attractive metaphor and not terribly practical.

Why were there no smaller companies among your examples?

The kinds of companies I work with are large multinationals, so I have a bias. But puppies, kittens, and young companies are agile as a birthright. They're naturally like that. It is the middle-aged and geriatric organizations that I am interested in. Smaller companies can get away with murder.

You reject the term "guru." Why is that?

I'm not a great guru or a repository of knowledge – that's the kiss of death. When you become a persona, you stop being a person, and that has a lot of costs. Jack Welch says he is as dumb as he is ever going to be. People think he is a guru manager and want to pick his brains, but he picks theirs. The best CEOs think like that.

What is the key question you ask when you go into an organization?

I go in the door under different guises – often as a consultant, sometimes as a researcher. I ask: What are your biggest strategic challenges and what are you doing about them? I let them talk to me about what they're doing, where they're going, and where there are hiccups. I try then to go deeper into the organization, beyond senior managers. I dig and dig until I start to hear enough of the same thing so I'm not surprised. If I do 16 to 20 interviews, I can get to the heart of what's going on inside an organization. I take notes and then, working inductively – I'm not deductive at all – I can abstract the themes. I let the data teach me – not the other way around.

[tom peters]

management liberator

a business mind who thinks the problem usually is...*management*

Tom Peters (born 1942) has cut a colorful, opinionated swathe through management thinking ever since the path-breaking publication of his 1982 book, *In Search of Excellence* (co-authored with Robert Waterman and published by Harper & Row).

Peters is a hugely charismatic person – on and off the seminar stage. His ebullient oratorical style tends to divide public opinion. People either love him or speedily question the depth of his thinking. Peters' intellectual rigor and freshness of perspective should not be so easily questioned. His first book was a huge bestseller – *In Search of Excellence* (1982, Harper & Row) ignited the business book market and created the modern guru whirl. But behind this, the book was studiously researched and its timing was impeccable. It struck the right note.

Peters' sequels have, at times, been disappointing. *Liberation Management* (1992, Knopf) stands out, however, as one of the most important business books of the 1990s. It set the organizational agenda and established benchmark companies. The agenda and the companies were then painstakingly picked over by others.

Peters' consulting career started in McKinsey, but he established his own firm just before the huge success of *In Search of Excellence*. For more information about Peters' career, go to *http://www.tompeters.com*.

In this interview, Peters looks at the genesis of his thinking and the development of his colorful career.

In Search of Excellence was the book that put you on the map. Of the many books you've written, has it turned out to be your favorite?

Definitely not. I was and am more pleased with *Liberation Management* than anything else I've ever written. It is a goldmine of information. It is basic reporting on research, reporting on theoretical stuff. I don't apologize for it. But it was also a self-indulgent book which should have been 40 percent shorter. It got the best and worst reviews I have ever got. Still, up to that point, *Liberation Management* was the only book I enjoyed writing.

Why did you enjoy it so much?

Liberation Management was the first time since *In Search of Excellence* I had really gone on the road to research things. At McKinsey, change was determined by charts and boxes. I wanted to get away from the hard S's so we ignored it. In *Liberation Management* I moved on to structure. The result changed the dialog a little bit. People hadn't looked at those companies. If I had to go back I wouldn't change it. Now, business book after book is working over the companies in *Liberation Management*.

Do you have a "least favorite"?

That would probably be *A Passion for Excellence* (1985, Collins). It truly is hopelessly disorganized. It came from me talking to zillions of people and doing seminars. Oddly enough, people – practitioners – still come up to me to say it is their favorite book. People read it for the sound bites.

How has *In Search of Excellence* held up?

The base of the case remains the same. Our conclusions have largely stood the test of time: a bias for action; close to the customer; autonomy and entrepreneurship; productivity through people; hands-on, values driven; stick to the knitting; simple form, lean staff; and, simultaneous loose-tight properties. The book, research, and companies have all taken some heat over the years, but the conclusions still resonate as logical and consistent.

Two years after publication, *BusinessWeek* ran its famous "Oops!" headline, and went on to reveal that the companies featured in the book were anything but excellent. I wouldn't disagree that I had been on the road too much. *BusinessWeek* was a great wake-up call. The article claimed that about a quarter of the "excellent" companies were struggling. That was an undeniable fact, and we started to get beaten up, badly. It was a very bad week. I didn't know what the answer was then, and I still don't know what the answer is. I do know, however, that *In Search of Excellence's* eight principles have survived intact – just the companies haven't.

Do bad reviews or other criticism bother you?

Everybody has a different tolerance level for criticism. Bob Waterman has the ability to not allow the barbs to affect him. He has Teflon™ skin. I smile a lot, but every wound is fatal. *In Search of Excellence* was a roller-coaster ride. *The Wall Street Journal* and *Fortune* loved it; The *New York Times, Harvard Business Review*, and *LA Times* savaged it. I am competitive to the core, and even though my main source of competition is with myself, I am still devastated when I get bad reviews. I've been beaten up by journalists about my work and my mission. My mission is to amuse myself. And for that, I will take some criticism.

Did the success of *In Search of Excellence* surprise you?

Consultants live with problems. That's what they get paid for. So we were always working with broken things. *In Search of Excellence* was the first book written about things that work. Admittedly, the logic of the book was an upfront attack on American management and McKinsey thinking. Okay, it was 75 percent about islands of hope, but that was what they were: exceptional. I consider *In Search of Excellence* a bad news book. It still amazes me to this day that it became a bestseller overseas. In 1987 I made my first trip to China. I was there for five weeks and met at least five different publishers who had bestselling editions of *In Search of Excellence*. It was a phenomenon, a Hula-Hoop. It's like being Neil Armstrong. It won't happen again, and it certainly won't happen to me again.

Consultants live with problems. That's what they get paid for

But success often comes with a price.

I really got beaten up by the *In Search of Excellence* experience. A lot of it in retrospect was very painful. Success can administer a bizarre beating – I never expected two pages about me in *People* magazine. It was a bewildering experience. I'm glad it happened, but in retrospect I would sooner be dropped into the ocean with a rock attached to me than go through it all again. It took me six years to get over it, though you never really get over anything. It was a ridiculously distorting process.

In spite of your successes as author, consultant, teacher, and speaker, you've been criticized as being inconsistent.

When I look at my output, I see that my books could be by different authors. I have no patience with consistency, and so regard the criticisms as a good thing. I consider inconsistency as a compliment. Perhaps the reason for my inconsistencies is that I don't set out to periodically rewrite the same books. I decide to write a new book when I feel disgusted and embarrassed by my previous one. So, it should not be surprising that my writing reflects changes in my thinking.

The right to change your mind is not a luxury given to every writer, especially business writers.

I am not a writer. I have too much respect for great writing to call myself that. In my field, I think I am a good writer, but that is not the same thing as being a writer. There is a fair hunk of me which is still an academic, and, when I went on sabbatical from McKinsey, I gave serious thought to teaching at Stanford and did teach there for two years as a lecturer. I have an enormous respect for research and am influenced greatly by the likes of Karl Weick, Ed Rapp, Brian Quinn, Herb Simon, and James March. My hero is Henry Mintzberg. They were the tiny minority of people looking at the disorderly, irrational side of management processes. I depended on their grounding. When I'm writing, I try to think whether the people who have influenced me would throw tomatoes at it or not. To some extent I am a translator who is good at finding interesting examples which make my topic relevant to people.

To some extent, that explains your fees, no?

In this regard we need to remember two things. First, I have worked a lot, for a long time, very hard. I found a calendar from 1985 recently and came close to vomiting. I was doing over 150 seminars a year at the time, sometimes doing two speeches in two different cities in the same day. I was either very strong or conned myself. I'm now working twice as hard tailoring the seminars. And, in spite of their often "tough love" look, they are done with genuine affection. I feel we are in the same boat.

Anything else we should remember?

Twenty years ago I was charging $1000 a speech, though after the book my speaking fees edged up to $2000 or $3000 and I had a couple of people working for me. I slept in one half of the apartment and worked in the other. One day I came back from a trip, and my assistant said I was speaking to Arthur Andersen and I was charging $10 000. They had asked what my fee was and she thought she would try $10 000. They agreed, and so my fee was now $10 000. My point is, I cash the checks, but it's nutty when people in India are making 25 cents an hour. I understand that there is something obscene about $100 000 a day. I'm comfortable with it when I'm rational. When I'm in India, I'm uncomfortable. I am not a bad economist, and I understand the market logic, the fee structure, and that's all we have here. Every year produces

another hero – Schwarzkopf, Ford, Kissinger, Thatcher, Powell – who sets the top of the market, and we glide in between them. That's how it works for all of us.

When you go into a company, what is the key question you ask?

Who are you?

[thomas petzinger, jr.]

new pioneer

a business mind facing the challenge of operating a real business

Though Tom Petzinger (born 1955) had written two books – *Oil & Honor* (1999, Beard Group), about the oil industry, and *Hard Landing* (1997, Times), about the airline industry – until 1999 most would have identified him as the lead management columnist for *The Wall Street Journal.* His "Front Lines" column was required reading for many executives for years.

Then Petzinger explored in depth the emergence of socially responsible (and highly successful) small business entrepreneurs. He identified the "new economy" before anyone else in the press was recognizing and reporting on it. His resulting book, *The New Pioneers* (1999, Simon & Schuster), not only awakened many big-company managers to the prospect of new ways of doing business, the writing experience even changed the author. In 2000, Petzinger decided to leave his journalistic roots and start a biotechnology enterprise in Pittsburgh, Pennsylvania.

Petzinger's work has been singled out by the *New York Times* for its "Notable Books" citation; he also won the coveted Gerald Loeb Award for Business and Financial Reporting. For more information, visit *http://www.launchcyte.com.*

In this interview, Petzinger discusses the new economy as he has researched it – and as he has now lived it.

When did you decide to leave authoring/speaking and become a new pioneer?

After leaving the *Wall Street Journal,* I realized it was time to become a more direct participant in the game I had been observing. It was time for me to try my hand at business. I was keen to involve myself in the convergence of life sciences and information sciences, which struck me as a very powerful trend. I wanted to apply directly the values and principles I had developed as a student of business. Also, frankly, it was the height of the new economy frenzy in the equities market, and new ventures were easy to fund. It seemed like a compelling time to make the leap. Little did I know that the funding scene would dry up just as I was taking the plunge!

How's it going? What have you learned?

Funding takes three times the time and effort I had imagined, but otherwise it's going well. I'm actually building a business on the principles I set out to build on, and that feels great. Even better, I can already see how doing so creates a return for the private capital invested in the business. We are actually *more* successful because we are honoring the humanity and dignity of the people we work with and serving to contribute to the betterment of the community and the betterment of human health.

That said, I am facing challenges that my earlier career did not prepare me for. The stress of daily journalism is nothing compared with the stress of building a business. When I was considering this transition, a wise entrepreneur I know told me I would learn things about myself in building a business that I would never otherwise realize. He was right, and I have to say I've not been pleased with everything I've learned.

Nonetheless, do you still believe that small business is where our future lies?

Yes. That's where most of the innovation and expansion are occurring. There will always be a place for big companies, of course. When a product or service becomes a commodity, then it's possible to compete only through price, and when cost is everything, economies of scale become critical. Look at the industries in the throes of today's mega mergers: oil, banking, retailing, telecommunications. They're all commodity-distribution industries where scale economies can still be obtained. But these megalithic industries account for a smaller and smaller proportion of economic activity. People talk about "the big getting bigger." Some of them are, but as a result the big are getting less numerous. The mega mergers are essentially the death throes of the dinosaurs.

The kind of natural teamwork that flourishes in small firms is also vital to big corporations

Anything that large corporations could learn from these pioneers?

Yes! The kind of natural teamwork that flourishes in small firms is also vital to big corporations. And in fact it flourishes in many big firms, in a number of large companies whose leaders have awakened to the need for a new workplace, one in which people collaborate and self-organize in natural, human ways. Lucent Technologies, for instance, has a plant in Mount Olive, New Jersey, where workers pick their own teams and invent their own work processes, and the place is startlingly productive.

But it's more than teamwork, right: you talk of "technologies, ideas, and values" as the cornerstones of this new breed of business leader.

One of the great paradoxes of the workplace and marketplace today is that technology is hastening a return to *traditional* values in business. Business was born in the home, and that's where it remained for virtually all of human existence; we called it the farm. Or look inside the walls of a traditional firm. Technology permits workers to self-organize and co-create – to seek out answers and to form working relationships as problems and opportunities arise. This breaks down the rigidity of traditional workplace structures. Before the industrial age, the division of labor and the formation of teams occurred naturally, and technology is rapidly returning us to that point.

Technology also drastically reshapes the marketplace, once again toward more traditional ways. Relational databases make it possible to treat prospects and customers as markets of one, in the same way that tailors, saddle-makers, and blacksmiths once worked. Communications technology permits direct contact with every customer, in the way the producers worked before the advent of mass media. One could look at technology today, since it's so pervasive, and say, "So, what's new?" Granted, automation technologies – typewriters, air compressors, even air travel – help people do more things (and make more things) better and faster. We've known that for some time. But communication technology helps people work qualitatively differently – ironically, in ways helping us become more human, not less.

However, large businesses use technology to communicate also.

Certainly some big companies are using technology in this more human way, but many, probably most, persist in using it to reinforce dehumanizing industrial-age structures. They use it to track individual performance in a Frederick Taylorist way. They use it to categorize and delimit working practices, which they pass off as "knowledge management." They use it to accelerate existing workflows – as a production-line speed-up – without considering new ways of doing the work.

On ideas, your book implies that larger companies are almost idea bankrupt. Is that what you think?

Not idea bankrupt maybe, but idea poor. Certainly, innovation is possible in big firms. Just look at 3M, Dupont, Monsanto, and Pfizer. But they're exceptions. Most firms are turning outside to acquire innovations. Microsoft has a voracious appetite for small companies. Fortunately, when big companies snap up small innovators they pay top dollar, which enables the small entrepreneur to create more new technologies, to found new firms, or to fund and mentor others doing the same.

On values, a lot of what makes these pioneers "new" is their choice of workstyles and lifestyles. Yet where's the concern for economic progress measured by indices such as return on investment or return on capital?

Most entrepreneurs want to build companies rather than milk them. Return on investment (ROI) is a meaningless metric to a lot of the best of them. Likewise return on capital: most of today's startups come into the world with hardly any capital at all. Creativity, not capital, is now the principal constraint in business formation. In a small, successful software firm, the return on capital tends toward the infinite, which makes it pretty much meaningless.

The new pioneers seem much more concerned about the connection between business and society. What are the long-range implications of that?

We would have better schools because business would realize that public education is integral to corporate success. We would have less crime and

Creativity, not capital, is now the principal constraint in business formation

smaller prison populations because work would be more fulfilling, motivating, and humanizing for all. We would have more harmonious racial relations because the celebration of diversity in the workplace would spill out into the community. We would have a better environment because business would see that it can't survive long by polluting the world in which it operates. I'm not being "pie in the sky" here. I have consistently reported for a long time on businesses engaged in precisely such initiatives. They are motivated by self-interest – but a form of self-interest that recognizes and honors their place in the communities around them.

Then if "new pioneer" values become the global standards in all businesses, would managers behave and act differently?

Yes, and I see at least three critical shifts. Number one: Managers must foster the maximum degree of contact possible between the workplace and the marketplace. This means making sure that *everyone* in the enterprise deals to some degree with customers, communities, investors – with every stakeholder. Number two: Senior executives, especially, need to quit marching to Wall Street's tune. Except in the case of utilities and strictly commodity businesses, quarterly earnings are utterly meaningless. When firms are brave enough to manage to their long term they free themselves from sacrificing real value – including social value – on the altar of today's stock price. Number three: though progress is already occurring, managers need to continue bridging the chasm they've long maintained between work life and family life. Whether this means telecommuting, flexitime, job sharing, workplace day care, decent health benefits, sick leave policies, better vacation schedules or even an end to nepotism restrictions depends on the circumstances. So much of the neurosis in the workplace and the family is due to the demands that each place on the other. We can, we are, bridging the gaps, but we've still got a long way to go.

[jeffrey pfeffer]

social scientist

a business mind who emphasizes people in the business equation

Jeffrey Pfeffer (born 1946) is the Thomas D. Dee II professor of Organizational Behaviour in the Graduate School of Business at Stanford University. He is the author or co-author of ten books, including *The Human Equation: Building Profits by Putting People First* (1998, Harvard Business School Press) and *The Knowing-Doing Gap: How Smart Companies Turn Knowledge into Action* (2000, HBS Press). His latest book is *Hidden Value: How Great Companies Achieve Extraordinary Results with Ordinary People* (2000, HBS Press). A common theme dominates Pfeffer's writing: that putting people first does not mean that business and profits have to suffer; in fact, he proves time and again that "human element" is often the source for extraordinary business performance.

Pfeffer serves on the boards of numerous companies; he is also a member of the visiting committee for Harvard Business School and on the advisory board for MTW Corporation, a software and computer consulting company. He has taught executive seminars in 26 countries in addition to lecturing in management development programs and consulting for many companies, associations, and universities in the United States. Pfeffer won the Richard D. Irwin award for Scholarly Contributions to Management as well as several awards for books and articles. For more information, log onto his Stanford Web site at *http://gobi.stanford.edu/faculty bios/bio.asp?ID=135.*

In this interview, Pfeffer delineates his strong view that people are the essence of organizations.

You seem fascinated by the human dimension in organizations. Why?

What other dimension is there to organizations, besides people? As an executive once said in a talk to my class: "Machinery and technology make it possible; people make it happen." The study of organizational behavior, the field in which I received my PhD, is rooted in psychology and social psychology, sociology, anthropology, and political science. All of these academic disciplines are based on the study of human behavior. It is only natural for those of us trained in organizational behavior to use that lens as we approach analyzing organizations in any country or any sector.

Although companies are fond of saying "people are our most important asset," when it comes to backing those words with action, few do

One senses that you feel that management has not maximised the value of the human element at work. What's causing that?

It's not just a matter of my opinion. McKinsey's "War for Talent" practice (and forthcoming book) speaks to what must happen for companies to attract and retain great people, and to the fact that relatively
few organizations do most of these things. My interview in *Fast Company* a few years ago brought numerous e-mails detailing the abusive
management practices common even in high-technology and know-
ledge-intensive sectors of the economy where they are terribly destructive to competitiveness. Although companies are fond of saying "people
are our most important asset," when it comes to backing those words
with action, few do. That means, by the way, that those companies that
actually put people first enjoy a tremendous competitive advantage.
There are many causes as to why companies haven't done what the
claim they want to do. Some blame Wall Street and its short-term focus.
Certainly there is little evidence that the typical Wall Street analyst, who
is relatively young and has never managed anything, understands
much about the human dimension of management. Another source of
the problem is measurements that confuse costs with investments,
training being a good example. Yet another source of difficulty is the
idea that good managers are "tough" managers, a legacy of the Al
Dunlap and Frank Lorenzo tradition that somehow refuses to die.

So the real problem is…

The most important part of the problem is philosophy and frame of
mind. Too many companies and their leaders see people as shirking,
effort-averse people who need to be controlled, measured, and moni-
tored. Too few see people as creative, curious, eager to learn, and willing to invest themselves in the company and its success if only they

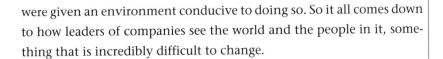

were given an environment conducive to doing so. So it all comes down to how leaders of companies see the world and the people in it, something that is incredibly difficult to change.

Yet no one reading your books would confuse them with "human resources" books; they all have a hard edge. Is that your intent?

I hope my readers will think, first of all. There is way too much "conventional wisdom" and unquestioned assumptions and ideology that guide management interventions. As a social scientist, I always try to provide data – not just case examples but systematic studies and evidence based on sound theory – for what I write about. I want people to question what they are hearing and reading and confront assertions with what we have learned over the years about individual and organizational behavior, which actually is quite a lot.

Companies and their leaders obviously need to learn and to be open to the environment, but they also need to put their own perspective and judgment to work

You're not fond of management fads, are you?

Many senior managers lack *courage* – the courage to tell the truth and to see things for what they are. This was certainly true during the so-called "new economy" or Internet boom in which simple common sense could tell you that much of what was being said was simply impossible, but it is true more generally. We have been enamored with benchmarking, but as I often point out, you cannot benchmark your way to the top (only to the middle). Everyone wants to earn exceptional returns but to do it by doing what everyone else is doing, which is simply impossible. There is almost too much information on what everyone else is doing which permits social influence to run rampant. Companies and their leaders obviously need to learn and to be open to the environment, but they also need to put their own perspective and judgment to work. Why should we pay huge executive salaries for people who simply imitate what others are doing or saying? Imitation should be much cheaper!

What will prove to be the most influential management idea of all time?

In some version, Douglas McGregor's Theory X and Theory Y, which is related to the self-fulfilling prophecy and other ideas about how to actually motivate and energize people.

What makes a management idea great?

It needs to be both true and useful. It turns out a lot of management ideas are neither.

When you get the chance to visit a new company, and you hear of some "great idea" for change, how do you evaluate what's "wheat" and what's "chaff"?

I ask two important questions: Can the great idea be successfully implemented? And does the idea solve a real problem for a real customer, in a cost-effective way?

Consider management in a larger context. How would you assess the profession of management now?

I think managers or leaders are no more than 50 percent as effective as they could be. In medicine, the Hippocratic oath has within it the admonition to first "do no harm." Many of the organizational practices of today, such as zero-sum performance ranking on a forced curve, individual pay for performance, excessive short-term measurements of outcomes rather than processes, and the pervasive use of fear-based management approaches, take potentially productive, intelligent people and create performance problems. This is not the fault so much of the individual managers as of the systems in which they are operating.

Is the academic training of managers doing its job as well as it could?

No. There is not nearly enough learning by doing, there is not nearly enough tolerance for mistakes, and there is not nearly enough individual-level development. Academic training is itself a business, and the economic model of getting more bodies in front of one instructor may make fiscal sense but does not do much for the ability to provide the individual-level coaching and mentoring experiences that are important for really mastering both conceptual material and skills.

What about the internal training of managers – all those corporate offsites, for example?

The problem here is that there is not enough connection between the offsite and what goes on back *on*site. Few training programs are evaluated by whether or not anything changes as a consequences. One of the things that measuring the knowledge-doing gap can do is help you evaluate training: if the training is working, people should be converging on a model of what affects performance *and* they should be implementing what they know on a more consistent basis.

What, then, keeps you so fully charged about building better managers and organizations?

Who knows? Natural curiosity, and a belief that things can be, and should be, better.

[c.k. prahalad]

core champion

a business mind who can embrace large corporations and the urban poor

C.K. Prahalad (born 1941, in India) was described in one journal as a "brilliant teacher." He is, of course, more than that. Prahalad may well be one of the most influential thinkers on corporate strategy today, with a special expertise on how companies can be imaginatively strategic.

Prahalad is co-author, with fellow professor Gary Hamel, of *Competing for the Future* (1994, Harvard University Press), named as a *BusinessWeek* Book of the Year in 1994. His 1990 co-authored essay on "core competence" is the *Harvard Business Review's* most reprinted article ever.

C.K. has ties to the University of Michigan Business School (where he is Harvey C. Fruehauf professor of business administration and professor of corporate strategy and international business) and to the Kenan-Flagler business school of the University of North Carolina at Chapel Hill.

When not teaching, he is chairman of PRAJA, the San Diego-based software company he co-founded (with Dr Ramesh Jain, also formerly of Michigan). The unique company name derives from a Sanskrit word for "people" and embodies C.K.'s life-long work of bridging the numerous gaps between disparate cultures and organizations through technology innovation and new business models. For more

information, log onto either *http://ww.praja.com* or *http://www.bus.umich.edu/academic/faculty/ckp.html*.

In this interview, Prahalad talks about consumers, corporations, and strategies.

How has the Internet helped redefine "consumer"?

The Internet is fundamentally transforming the underlying structures of companies and the way they do business. First of all, note that the Internet is not about dot.coms. Whether companies are Internet pure-plays or traditional companies moving onto the net, they will both morph into something very different. This is because of the transparency the Internet brings to consumers in terms of performance, pricing, and structures. This is creating a new relationship between companies and consumers which, compared with traditional broadcasting, is more like a conversation. Consumers, individually or in

What the Internet is doing is giving power to consumers, individually and in groups, and this will force companies to a consumer-centric approach

groups, can start a dialogue with companies. And they can – and will – expect to be included in the development of products and services.

What will be the impact of this new, active customer?

The result will be a fundamental shift in power from firms to consumers. Business will become consumer-centric rather than firm-centric. For example, companies talk a lot about customer relationship management, but that is really a firm-centric view. What the Internet is doing is giving power to consumers, individually and in groups, and this will force companies to a consumer-centric approach. A second impact which we see increasingly is that consumers are now interested in experiences – not in products or services *per se* – and companies will have to provide these.

You've also written about a very non-intuitive consumer base: people living in poverty.

Think about 4.5 billion people in the world who live in abject poverty. People talk about the digital divide, but I believe we can obtain a digital, or technological, dividend that will turn these people into active consumers. Traditionally we think that someone with an income of one or two dollars a day cannot be part of a market. I don't believe that. We say that the poor can't afford things. But that's really an assumption about our cost structures. We can't, or think we can't, produce and distribute goods at a price they can afford.

What got you thinking about this group?

About 10 or 12 years ago I began to question what was happening with the break-up of communism and the movement from "controlled" to emerging economies. Then I began to do some research in India, which to some extent I use as a proxy for the emerging economies of Eastern Europe, China, Indonesia, and so on. These are huge markets of billions of people who all suffer from the same problems. Often these markets have a tiny elite that is doing very well but a huge majority that is very poor. Western companies may be interested in the small, globally minded elite but ignore the majority. Yet these people want to join the market economy. But they can't because of the way it is structured.

The market is structured to reject potential consumers?

What happens is that the multinationals are looking after the rich and leaving the poor to be the concerns of the state. So the poor have become used to subsidies, which they cannot escape from to join the market economy. But that can't go on because developing countries cannot afford to continue the subsidies.

This is a complicated social and political problem. How is the market an answer?

I think there is an alternative solution that combines high technology, sustainable development, and changes in price performance. We have to create a market, to change our assumption of the poor as a burden to considering the poor as a commercial opportunity. Companies like Unilever and Citibank are already beginning to do this. For example, India Unilever can now deliver ice creams at just three cents each, and soon it will be two cents, because it has rethought the technology of refrigeration. Citibank can now provide financial services to people, also in India, who only have $25 a year to invest, again through rethinking the technology. And these businesses are vastly profitable.

So the key to helping the poor is technology?

Yes. High-tech allows you to aggregate markets cheaply so that, though individually consumer spending may be tiny, overall it is very profitable. But it's not just the technology, it's also about rethinking cost and price structures.

You are well known for your ideas regarding organizational cost and structure, and the need to reengineer. Recently, though, you've revised some of those earlier beliefs.

As you know, in the past 20 years hundreds of companies have downsized dramatically. In the process, while many have gained efficiency, too often companies end up losing competencies that reside in the masses of people cut without sufficient cause. I believe that if you

For my money, a growth orientation around core competencies stands the greatest chance of making market sense

repeat the restructuring process more than two or three times, what happens in the end is not only do you cut some fat but you also start losing muscle. Corporate anorexia develops, leading to total weakness.

Companies should think "grow" rather than "cut"?

That's what the idea of "core competencies for growth" is all about. The best way for a company to grow is to build growth into its strategy. You can downsize and reengineer processes until you become more efficient. When you go to work the next day, you will still be in the same business, but you will not have created anything new. Ultimately, it is the market which will decide what makes the best business sense. For my money, a growth orientation around core competencies stands the greatest chance of making market sense.

But are you anti-reengineering?

No. It has its place. But it must not become the sole and exclusive focus of management. So don't interpret my comments as saying that reengineering is no good. Within certain limits it is a good remedy. Sometimes it is a necessary condition, but it is seldom enough.

Reengineering is relatively safe. Growth entails risk. How do you reconcile the two?

Well, if you think of strategy as a packet of value creation, the question is less about assuming risks and more about grabbing chances. What companies need to do is discover new ways of leveraging resources, their own and those of their partners and allies, suppliers, clients, and competitors. The problem is how you share those risks and how you leverage resources. That is terribly important, especially for small companies, because they cannot afford to lose on big risks. When one bad mistake may be fatal, I would not suggest "take every risk." I am saying, ask how to grab chances and eliminate the risks associated with them.

Risk taking is less a part of many company's learning curves than are cutbacks, recisions, and reengineering.

It isn't that learning curves aren't helpful. Of course they are. However, when change is discontinuous, the learning based on previous experience is not enough by itself. You have to learn to forget. When there is a discontinuous change, as is the case today, there are enormous problems not only in the learning of new things but also in forgetting the old ones. Instead of talking about the curve of learning, I would rather talk about the curve of forgetting.

[jonas ridderstråle]

funkster

a business mind who asserts that being different is a definite plus

Jonas Ridderstråle (born 1966, in Sweden) is an anomaly in the buttoned-down business world. Along with his co-author, friend, and associate, Kjell Nordström, Ridderstråle doesn't wear suits to business presentations, prefers to keep his head shaved, wears only black, and calls his lectures "gigs." *TIME* called the pair "radical prophets of consumerism," which is apt.

Ridderstråle burst into international prominence with *Funky Business: Talent Makes Capital Dance* (2000, ft.com), co-written with Nordström. The book was an international bestseller and argues that diversity, innovation, uncertainty, and change need to be constantly sought out – and capitalized on. "To succeed, we must stop being so goddam normal," they assert in the book. "If we behave like all the others, we will see the same things, come up with similar ideas, and develop identical products or services."

Ridderstråle is an assistant professor at the Stockholm School of Economics. For more information, go to *http://www.funkybusiness.com/funky/*.

In this interview, Ridderstråle shows how his ability to "e-magine" the future of business has elevated him to such prominence as a business thinker.

Why do you suggest that companies invest in imagination?

When you invest in raw materials, like a mine or an oil field, there is only one thing that you can be absolutely, 100 percent sure about: sooner or later, you are going to run out of that stuff. But when you invest in human imagination – feelings and fantasy – the sky is the limit. There is no end. And so, limitless leverage is possible.

Where does this "imagination capital" come from?

Don't expect too much innovation at a company where 90 percent of the employees are of the same gender, are about the same age, come from a similar educational background, and dress the same way, even if they go on bi-annual strategy conferences to the Mediterranean to be really creative, wild, and crazy. Companies need to attract talent, and talent is not only the preserve of middle-aged, white males with an MBA. The diversity game is played from the neck up, not the waist down. In nature, diversity is necessary in order to produce mutations that ensure survival. In business, diversity is a prerequisite for innovation that results in temporary monopolies. But of course you have also got to let these guys work together in teams. There is no mutation without mating. Then, companies need to realize that talent is not their greatest asset but a gigantic liability. Unless they can transform it into structural capital, by codifying and communicating it throughout the organization, talent belongs to the core competents – the people who make competencies happen.

The potential might be there at many firms; more likely, though, companies are going to have to think differently about everything they do, from hiring to development to markets to marketing, in order to accomplish the innovation necessary to be competitive in an Internet-

based, global economy. As traditional companies also become e-businesses, they will have to think very differently.

But isn't creativity assumed to characterize most e-business, almost by definition?

Unfortunately, in laudable efforts to avoid bureaucracy, many e-businesses have opted for anarchy. But creativity does not thrive in an anarchic environment. Companies need a set of key principles around which they organize creativity and creatively. Increasingly, values will constitute this lowest common denominator, allowing for variation in other dimensions and clearing the way for self-organization. Firms must become tribes. How do you get people to share your values? Short answer: find those who already do. Look at Hell's Angels or Greenpeace. Just imagine Hell's Angels hiring for skills! "We hire attitudes," says Herb Kelleher, CEO of Southwest Airlines. The logic is that you can

How do you get people to share your values? Short answer: find those who already do

make positive people into good pilots, but turning great pilots with attitude problems into charming servers of customers is close to impossible.

Today we see successful companies recruiting people with the right attitude, then training them in skills – not the reverse. There are two good reasons for this. Number one, because the half-life of knowledge is coming down so fast that if you recruit someone with relevant knowledge today, three months down the road when he or she starts, this competence may be obsolete. Number two, most of us have a whole lot easier time changing our skills than our values. We are talking about a major mind-shift here. In one important respect, an e-market is the same as a traditional market. Not all companies will win (kind of obvious). What makes this situation so special is that the forces against winning are particularly strong on the net, with informed customers and competitors just clicks away. And today there are just too many plain vanilla-flavored e-business companies incapable of self-renewal out there. In the long run, intelligence and intangibles are the only possible remedies.

Intelligence and intangibles?

The intelligence to understand that we have moved into an age of abundance, a surplus society. In 2000, consumers in Europe could choose between 1500 bank sites; publishers put out 2000 new business books alone and 30 000 new CDs; and US grocery stores stocked 20 000 items. The average consumer faces 247 advertisements daily. Abundance is a fact of our lives, meaning we have more choices than ever. The only trouble is that *more* quite often simply means more of the same. Products have become increasingly homogenous. Those companies that win will be smart enough to see the importance of intangibles. And the most important intangible of all, the key innovation necessary, is entering the emotional economy.

What is the emotional economy?

Consider the Finnish company Nokia, which has come from almost nowhere to become the leading maker of mobile phones in the world. Why has this firm been so successful? Nokia does not possess ground-breaking technology which its competitors cannot get hold of. Nor has its CEO, Jorma Olilla, stumbled upon a marketing book yet to be translated from Finnish. In fact, Nokia must have world-class, top-of-the-line technology. It must pioneer organizational solutions. The company needs the best IT solutions that money can buy. It must work with the best suppliers in the world, not the closest. All this is necessary. There is no choice. But, it is not enough, because Ericsson is also doing it. Motorola is doing it. They are all doing it.

True competitiveness must instead be built around something we all know exists but which is seldom discussed in the business world: emotions and imagination. A company must develop sensational strategies that capture the attention of its tribe. In the past, strategies did not target emotions; today they must. Attracting the emotional customer and colleague is not a question of superior price or performance. This is necessary but not sufficient. Ethics and aesthetics have little to do with logic, but everything to do with feelings and fantasy.

Emotional business is an alternative way of communicating and reasoning with consumers. In an age of abundance and information overload, where attention is a scarce resource, organizations have to ask if they are really getting through. Are they striking the right keys, or is something lacking? Most organizations could load their messages with more feelings. Instead of just reasoning with people it is time to appeal to their affection, intuition, and desire.

How does a company optimize emotional experiences?

Well, what about adding elements of aesthetics and entertainment (A&E)? If all customer offerings contain an aesthetical element, and they do, we should consider them as pieces of art. Where is art displayed? At museums and galleries. Visit MoMa in New York and learn something about the shop of the future. It sure as hell seems as if the Pradas and Guccis of the world have done it. Just look at how the products are displayed at their stores. Want to add some entertainment? Go to an amusement park. Look at how much people seem to enjoy themselves at a Sharper Image store – and they are smiling all the way to the cash register. Focus or combine A&E, but please do something. Move it or become Pompei-fied – the shop of the future is a museum, in more respects than one.

That's putting the case rather strongly.

That's because the message is so important. Executives either start thinking differently or they will watch their companies go away. Companies are disposable – that's the bottom line. If, for one reason or another, CBS goes down the drain, it's not detrimental to David Letterman. If Alessi goes bankrupt, designer Jasper Morrison may shed a tear, but he will soon be back on track. If Harvard Business School has to close down the store, Professor Michael Porter just moves on. If Sony music is teetering on the abyss, Madonna is unlikely to have sleepless nights. In an age where capital is abundant, the bargaining power of Dave, Jasper, Michael, and Mrs Ritchie is increasing by the hour, by the minute, by the second.

Human beings are not commodity goods. We differ. Firms either manage this differentiation or watch their most precious assets walk out of the door. To recruit and retain great people we have to treat them

as individuals. It used to be XM (extra medium). Now it has to be XME. The consequence is that each and every little system needs to be personalized. Perhaps, instead of being provided with detailed job descriptions, employees should provide managers with motivation descriptions. Human beings are emotional rather than rational creatures. Yet reasoning is what the typical manager is rewarded for. Eventually the analytical side of the brain grows so large and heavy that some executives find it difficult to avoid walking in circles. These lawyers and MBAs and engineers forget that "e" doesn't stand for electronic; "e" stands for emotion. Think emotional capital. Stir emotions in your consumers and colleagues.

This strategy will create a more loyal customer base? Is that what you've meant in your discussions of "tribes"?

The consequences of digitization, deregulation, and globalization are increasing marketification + product homogenization + capacity

Think emotional capital. Stir emotions in your consumers and colleagues

expansion + perfect information = perfect competition. In such a world, firms risk ending up as price takers. Marginal revenues will just about cover marginal costs. The basic conditions for a shift where power is transferred from those who sell to those who buy are here. Forget about kings and queens. The new customer is a demanding dictator. Companies will have to do business with the consumer equivalent of Saddam Hussein. And right now, he may very well be on the Web, trying to link up with Augusto Pinochet and Muammar al-Qaddafi to use their collective bargaining power. The stupid, humble, loyal customer who was bullied by companies in a world where demand mostly exceeded supply is about to die. So, the companies that stand the best chance of surviving in the e-marketplace are those that identify and find a neat niche, a funky few, a global tribe. You need to understand your particular tribe better than anyone else. You must know what makes them tick, what scares them, what gets them out of bed in the morning, what turns them on. The tribe is the basic unit of business. If you don't know who your tribe is or anything about them, you are not going to stand out from the crowd. Also remember, your tribe must be a consequence of who you are.

Niche markets and tribes sound like minimal financial returns on large investments.

The good news is that there are a lot of tribes out there, and some are enormous. Consider this example from the already saturated world of financial services. The American Steve Dunlap was refused a loan to build a resort for homosexuals. So he decided to establish the G&L Internet Bank. The basic idea is to target the 21 million or so American gays and lesbians – a group with a combined annual budget of some $800 billion. Niche markets and tribes change our understanding of what it takes to be good.

You're really saying that being "good," in the traditional sense, is no longer good enough.

Good used to depend on location and having merchandise in stock. Location now is any person's home computer, and stock is unlimited, because choice is unlimited. If you focus your energy on creating and then exploiting an extremely narrow niche, you can make a lot of money. The tribe may consist of one-legged homosexual dentists. It may be lawyers who race pigeons. But if you manage to capture these customers globally, you can make a lot of money. There are riches in niches.

Is there a way to characterize the revised rules for success in the new economy?

A start-up or an existing company will need to follow four rules. First, build an organizational tribe. Your employees need to believe in the company. Tom Peters noted that women make some 65 percent of all car-buying decisions in the US. Yet a mere 7 percent of all car sales people are women, men design virtually all cars, and men dominate the managerial echelons of car companies. This is not only a question of equality, it is a question of quality of decisions and customer offerings. The easiest way to build a tribe, of course, is to hire the right people from the outset, and then train them.

The second rule?

Extend the tribe biographically. The world of yesterday was geographically structured, and so were its tribes. The new tribes – whether they are Hell's Angels, computer nerds, Amnesty International, or the Peoples Republic of Britney Spears – are biographically structured. They are global tribes of people who feel they have something in common, no matter where they were born. What does matter is that the targetted tribe has a common bond – values and attitudes – with your organizational tribe.

The third rule?

Identify and involve individuals. Within a tribe there must be room for personalization and individual differences. Companies must, as a result, deal with micro markets of single individuals and extreme diversity. Companies must customize, then customize still further. 3M's Post-it notes now come in 18 colors, 27 sizes, 56 shapes, and 20 fragrances. Truck-maker Scania created modularized trucks which allow customers to build their personal truck – cafeteria style. Barbie comes complete with 15 000 combinations.

But total customization involves more than the customer offering – it must encompass the entire experience. While American artist Barbara Kruger may be capturing the gist of our super-capitalist society with the

The only way to create real profit is to attract the emotional rather than the rational consumer

slogan "I shop – therefore I am," people not only desire shopping to express their individuality and tribal belonging, they also want to avoid too much complexity. Innovative organizations help people to avoid information overload and aid them in making smart choices. Either companies focus on internally producing this service – by employing experts, aggregating information, and comparing prices such as Pricerunner.com – or as at Amazon.com they choose to more actively involve the consumers in the process.

The fourth rule?

Replace the rational with the emotional. The only way to create real profit is to attract the emotional rather than the rational consumer. If you try reasoning, you will have to deal with the purely economic rationality of the demanding customer. This inevitably results in zero profits as you will compete globally with an infinite number of other similar firms. Steve Jobs of Apple was recently asked about what makes the new Mac OS X operating system so great. He replied: "We made the buttons on the screen look so good you'll want to lick them." Not a single word about megahertz and gigabytes. Such companies understand that although economies of scale and skill still matter, the new game is one of economies of soul.

profit

A good case in point is Harley-Davidson. The company is not just sell-ing a motorcycle, it is selling American nostalgia. The arguments for buying a Harley have little to do with rational reasoning – price, per-formance, etc. – and everything to do with affection, intuition, and desire. Or as a Harley exec once put it: "What we sell is the ability for a 43-year-old accountant to dress in black leather, ride through small towns, and have people be afraid of him." Harley-Davidsons symbolize feelings of freedom and independence, feelings that people want in a stressful world.

In an age of abundance with more or less endless choice for consumers, success is contingent on capturing the emotional human being. So, do you *love* – not like or fancy, love – your products, colleagues, and cus-tomers? Are they passionate about you? The real acid test: during the past two years, how many of your customers have tattooed your brand on one of their biceps? If Harley-Davidson can get its tribal followers to do it, so can you. Sounds too touchy-feely? Well, even research in neuroscience shows that the brain's limbic system, which governs our feelings, is way more powerful than the neocortex that controls intel-lect. The traffic instructions that evolution provided our brains with are pretty clear: emotions have the right of precedence. Logic just has to wait.

If you go into a company, what's the most important question you ask?

> If some strange force were to wipe your company off the face of planet earth, what would the world miss out on?

What question would you like to ask the managers of the world?

> Replace your company with you in the question above.

[al ries]

focussed strategist

a business mind who's focussed on marketing, strategy, and branding

Al Ries (born 1926) invented the concept of "positioning" 20 years ago, after working for twice that long in major corporations around the world. He co-authored (with Jack Trout) *the* book on the subject, *Positioning: The Battle For Your Mind* (1993, Warner). And in many ways, that battle has captivated Ries – and his legions of followers – ever since.

Ries has always felt that, in an overcrowded marketplace, the best path to success is to focus on an area in which your company can innovate and excel. He has authored or co-authored some of the most successful marketing books of all time: *Marketing Warfare* (with Trout, 1997, McGraw Hill), *Focus: The Future of Your Company Depends on it* (1997, HarperBusiness), *Bottom-up Marketing* (with Trout, 1990, Plume), *The 22 Immutable Laws of Branding* (1998, Harper), as well as *The 11 Immutable Laws of Internet Branding* (2000, HarperBusiness). Of his many books, it's not unusual to find reader reviews which exclaim that Ries "without question changed the way we run our business."

In 1999, Ries was included in the list of the 100 most influential public relations people of the 20th century by *PR Week*. He has also featured prominently in *BusinessWeek, The Wall Street Journal,* the *Los Angeles Times,* and the *New York Times*.

The first advertising agency founded by Ries opened in New York in the 1960s. That company became the famous Trout & Ries firm. In 1994, Ries founded Ries & Ries with his daughter, Laura; they operate their firm out of Atlanta. For more information, go to *http://www.alries.com*.

In this interview, Ries provides an overview of marketing and branding, with some special comments about the advent of the Internet and how that is changing strategy.

What is the secret of long-term corporate success?

The best opportunity for long-term success lies in narrowing the focus. For example, Motorola was the pioneer in mobile phones, but the company itself got into a wide variety of products and services including semiconductors, computers, and satellite communications systems. Nokia, on the other hand, took the opposite approach. It used to make a wide variety of products including computers, tires, paper, chemicals, and electronics. Then it decided to focus on mobile phones.

And who came out ahead?

Compare Motorola with Nokia. Motorola is the larger company, with sales in 2000 of $31 billion compared with Nokia with sales of $20 billion. But Nokia is a far more valuable company, with higher profits and a more powerful brand name. According to Interbrand, the brand strategy consulting group, the Nokia brand is worth $38.5 billion, and the Motorola brand is worth only $3.6 billion. Today Nokia is the worldwide leader in mobile phones, with 28 percent of the market compared with Motorola with 16 percent.

But which would most companies like to be?

Would you rather be Nokia or Motorola? The astonishing fact is that some 99 percent of business leaders would rather be Motorola. How do we know this? Not by what they say, but by what they do. The emphasis in most companies is expansion rather than contraction. Typical questions that business leaders ask themselves are: "What else can we get into? How do we extend our brand? How do we capitalize on the equity we have in our brand name? What companies can we merge with that will provide a good fit with our product line?" Why company leaders act this way in the face of overwhelming evidence to the contrary is the question I'm currently exploring.

What is your research showing thus far?

That companies, like individuals, fall into a common and predictable trap. Consider four examples to see my point. *One*: you are the hottest star on prime-time television. You make the most money; you have the highest ratings. So what do you do next? Of course. You open on Broadway as the star of *Macbeth*. The show lasts just ten performances. If Kelsey Grammer can fall into the trap, so can you. *Two*: you are the most famous basketball player in the world. You make the most money; you have the best reputation. So what do you do next? Of course. You try out for a different sport. You try out for baseball and naturally fail to make the Big Leagues. If Michael Jordan can fall into the trap, so can you. *Three*: you are the most famous copier company in the world. You make the most money; you have the best reputation. So what do you do next? Of course. You get into the computer business and you lose a bundle of money. If Xerox can fall into the trap, so can you. *Four*: you are the most famous computer company in the world. You make the most money; you have the best reputation. So what do you do next? Of course. You get into the copier business and you lose a bundle of money. If IBM can fall into the trap, so can you.

Your examples make a pretty compelling case.

What is it about people, about companies, about organizations? In their desire to grow, to get better, to get richer, they all make the same mistake. They all fall into the same trap. The trap is the biggest mistake you will ever make in your own career. You will try to grow by expansion rather than by contraction.

How do we avoid the trap?

If you are like most people, you keep asking yourself the wrong question! You keep asking yourself, what else? What else can I get into? What else can I do with my life? What else is out there that I am missing out on? What you are missing out on is the secret of life itself. You win by contracting, by narrowing your focus. By being a big fish in a small pond and then by making that small pond a lot bigger. Not by being a small fish in a big pond and then getting eaten by one of the

What is it about people, about companies, about organizations? In their desire to grow, to get better, to get richer, they all make the same mistake

big fish. What else can you do? You can do less. You can literally change your life overnight by doing less and by narrowing your focus. That's the way to avoid "the trap."

What got you thinking along these lines?

Virtually every client we work with asks us the same question: "How do we extend the brand into new products and markets?" Or they phrase it as more of a practical issue: "What are we going to do about the Internet?"

What advice should we heed about the Internet?

For your business, is the Internet a medium, or is it a business? Every company should be using the Internet as a communications medium. You should no more ignore the net than you would ignore the fax or the phone.

And if the net is going to be a business?

On the other hand, if the net is going to be a business, then you have some serious thinking to do. Generally you should start with a clean sheet of paper and design the business for the Internet, including giving your new Internet business a different name. Look at the big successes on the Internet. Yahoo, AOL, Priceline.com, eBay, Amazon.com. None of them is a line extension of an existing brand. And for the most part, these businesses do not have real-world counterparts. They are truly businesses designed to take advantage of the incredible "interactivity" of the Internet.

They also were "firsts."

Even if they weren't, that wouldn't necessarily have been a problem. All you have to do to be a leader is to narrow the focus. Instead of competing head to head with Amazon, a site called VarsityBooks.com is in the process of becoming the leader in textbooks. Ditto for a site called Alibris.com that is aiming to become the leader in used books.

Should companies seriously consider moving their business from the real world to the Internet?

They should give this question some serious thought. Maybe they should take the plunge like Charles Schwab, Dell Computer, and Cisco Systems. Each of these companies is committed to moving its business pretty much in its entirety to the net. If so, then you can keep your same name. If you try to do both – that is, keep a real-world business and an Internet business going under the same name – you are asking for trouble. You are going to have pricing problems, stocking problems, and a whole range of difficulties. You have a pretty basic choice, really. You can ignore the Internet or you can embrace the Internet. Either strategy can work. What won't work is trying to straddle the Internet.

[peter senge]

learning organizer

a business mind who advanced the learning organization

Peter Senge (born 1947) is widely known for *The Fifth Discipline: The Art and Practice of the Learning Organization* (1990, Doubleday), a book that has become "the Bible" for managers seeking to convert new knowledge into organizational improvement. The *Harvard Business Review* tagged the book as seminal to modern management thinking. As one biographical profile states: "Dr Senge's work articulates a cornerstone position of human values in the workplace; namely, that vision, purpose, reflectiveness, and systems thinking are essential if organizations are to realize their potentials."

Senge holds degrees in engineering and social systems modeling; his doctorate is in management. He is on the faculty of the Massachusetts Institute of Technology and is chairperson of the Society for Organizational Learning (SOL).

Senge also collaborated on two related books. He co-authored *The Fifth Discipline Fieldbook: Strategies and Tools for Building a Learning Organization* (1994, Nicholas Brealey) and *The Dance of Change: The Challenges to Sustaining Momentum in Learning* (1999, Doubleday). For more information about him, log onto *http://www.solonline.org/com/peo/psenge.html*.

In this interview, Senge discusses the importance of converting learning into vision, purpose, and systems thinking.

What is a "learning organization"?

In the simplest sense, a learning organization is a group of people who are continually enhancing their capability to create their own future. The traditional meaning of the word learning is much deeper than just taking in information. It is about changing individuals so that they produce results they care about – accomplish things that are important to them.

What are the components of a learning organization?

There are five essential components. The first is personal mastery. For organizations to grow, survive, thrive, and learn, familiar competencies and skills associated with management are necessary but insufficient. True learning also necessitates spiritual growth – opening oneself up to a progressively deeper reality – and living life from a creative rather than a reactive viewpoint. This discipline involves two underlying movements: continually learning how to see current reality more clearly, and learning from the ensuing gap between vision and reality which produces the creative tension that makes learning possible.

The second component?

The second component, mental models, goes hand in hand with personal mastery. This deals essentially with the organization's driving and fundamental values and principles. Managers must remain alert to the power of patterns of thinking at the organizational level which play themselves out without the awareness of organizational members. This component also highlights the importance of non-defensive inquiry into the nature of these patterns.

The third component of a learning organization?

The third component is shared vision. By this I mean the overlap between joint and personal visions. Shared vision can only be built on personal vision – a joint creation of organizational members. Shared vision is present when the task that follows from the vision is no longer seen by the team members as separate from the self.

What is the fourth component?

Team learning. The discipline of team learning involves two practices: dialogue and discussion. The former is characterized by its exploratory nature, the latter by the opposite process of narrowing down the field to the best alternative for the decisions that need to be made. The two are mutually complementary, but the benefits of combining them only come from having previously separated them. Most teams lack the ability to distinguish between the two and to move consciously between them.

The final component?

That is systems thinking – essentially, recognizing that things are interconnected. Organizations are complex systems, full of patterns, connections, and interdependencies. Managers who understand the nature of systems are better able to spot repetitive patterns, such as the way certain kinds of problems persist, or the way systems have their own built-in limitations to growth.

These components imply a significant change in the job of management.

For the traditional organization, the learning organization poses huge challenges. In the learning organization managers are researchers and designers rather than controllers and overseers. Managers should encourage employees to be open to new ideas, communicate frankly with each other, understand thoroughly how their companies operate, form a collective vision, and work together to achieve their goal. This is hard to do and certainly is not the way most managers were taught to do things. I know people who have lost their jobs supporting these theories.

Where did your ideas come from?

It happened over the course of 15 years. Each of those disciplines represents a significant body of theory and management methods, some

In the learning organization managers are researchers and designers rather than controllers and overseers

going back 100 years. What was new in designing this picture of five disciplines was understanding how there was synergy between them. In particular the Fifth Discipline – systemic thinking – expresses the sensibility that integrates all the others. In my opinion, all are different perspectives of an independent and dynamic vision of the world, in which human beings have the capacity to co-create their future.

Is the learning organization and Fifth Discipline philosophy – or management?

The core theories of these disciplines are profound. For example, the discipline of the personal domain has its roots in the Old Testament – "where there is no vision the people die." As another example, the basic idea of team learning involves the practice of dialogue, which has its birth in the Greek dialogue, that literally means "chain of ideas," that is, what is created when a group of people talk among themselves in a way that promotes a flow of ideas between them. The principles spring from ideas rooted in Judea-Christian religions, Buddhism, and Confucianism. So, with these fundamentals, the five disciplines have their roots both in philosophy and in practice.

Non-American management has had some difficulty accepting this type of discourse. Do you think that the Fifth Discipline and learning organization are American management buzzwords that will not catch on in other parts of the world?

You cannot talk about "buzzword" in relation to something which has its basis in the progression of human history. And there has been a growing interest in Europe in developing the learning capacities of organizations. The Society for Organizational Learning that I helped to establish and that connects organizations, researchers, and consultants

has spread through several European countries, for example in the United Kingdom, Holland, France, Scandinavia, and Germany.

Is the Fifth Discipline a management revolution?

If these changes permeate all the "tissue" of the organization, not just the economics of business, then we will see a mutation in the organizational DNA. But in this mutation process the five disciplines are only a step. Without any doubt, other tools, methods, and theories will develop and integrate themselves in a repertoire of management and leadership of the post-industrial age.

If an organization were going to be at the forefront of such a revolution, what competencies would management be trying to build?

The organizations with more willingness to learn achieve it by developing competencies in the areas of aspiration, reflection, and the understanding of complexity. These are three nuclear competencies. They are not characteristics. There is a background difference here that is not merely semantic. Characteristics are, in the common sense of management, things that can be identified and that others can copy. By nuclear competencies, I mean something different that develops with the years, by a persistent effort. It is a process, not a product. The learning organization is not an instantaneous solution.

What are some examples of best practices in organizational learning?

To tell the truth, I hesitate in identifying what you ask. Identifying "best practices" tends to prompt organizations to copy more than to understand. The root of all innovation is the theory and the method, not the practice. Don't get me wrong. Best practices are, without a doubt, important, but they are always situational. They always develop as a consequence of the capacities of a group of people facing specific circumstances. That is why trying to clone the best practices is almost always disappointing. Nobody learns how to build planes studying the best practices of the aeronautic industry. The theory of aerodynamics is the basis for building planes, as other theories are in relation to other domains of human activity, in arts, sciences, and technology.

But in the SOL network, aren't there examples that are worth studying?

Without any doubt. The organizational members of SOL are real, living labs for the development of better theory and methods. For example, both BP and Shell are making big changes – what Shell called transformation – having in mind the leadership of the oil industry in the coming years. Other interesting examples are being done in AT&T,

The root of all innovation is the theory and the method, not the practice

Harley-Davidson, Intel, HP, Federal Express, and many other members of the SOL community.

Is knowledge management the same thing as organizational learning?

No. In my opinion, knowledge management is at the same time a buzz-word and a set of profound ideas. The buzzword will certainly disappear, as all fashions do. But the background issues about the generation and diffusion of knowledge will be the target of the vanguard organizations for many years, but only when they learn to distinguish information from knowledge. Many consultants and many responsible people inside organizations are treating knowledge as if it were a special type of information. That's why you see a very strong tendency to use information technology in managing knowledge processes. This is a big confusion, and if it is not reconciled, knowledge management efforts will lack the good practical results necessary to motivate management to continue knowledge management initiatives.

[patricia seybold]

customer champion

a business mind who puts online customer relationships first

Patricia Seybold (born 1949) has been a computer industry consultant for more than 20 years and is founder of the Patricia Seybold Group, a worldwide strategic technology consulting and research group located in Boston.

Seybold shot to thought-leader status on the back of her 1998 bestselling book, *Customers.com: How to Create a Profitable Strategy for the Internet and Beyond* (co-authored with colleague Ronni Marhsak and published by Times Books). The book provided insight into how leading companies design their e-business strategies to achieve greater revenue, profitability, and customer loyalty.

"What's the formula for success?" Seybold asked. "Make it easy for customers to do business with you!" At a time when many companies were struggling to understand e-commerce, the message was simple, "It's the customers, stupid!" and Seybold delivered it with aplomb. (Seybold is living proof of what online sales can do; she says that more than half of the 300 000 copies sold were purchased via online booksellers like Amazon.)

Her follow-on book, *The Customer Revolution: How to Thrive When Your Customers Are in Control* (2001, Crown), focusses on the fact that metrics of customer satisfaction and loyalty are replacing the old yardsticks of sales per square foot and profit margins. In the book, Seybold takes her message to a wider audience – beyond technology managers to senior managers and financial analysts. Her aim, she says, is to educate them and the investment community as a whole about the long-term impact of customer loyalty on profitability. For more information, log onto *http://www.psgroup.com*.

In this interview, Seybold explains why she believes today's economy gives more power to customers than ever before.

Your first book, *Customers.com,* was all about making it easy for customers to do business with you online. What is the key message of your new book?

I noticed that nobody understood what was going on in this so-called "new economy." I believe that the current economy isn't a high-tech economy, nor an Internet economy, nor an m-commerce economy, but instead a *customer* economy. Customers, armed with information and access, are much more demanding than ever before. They are demanding fair, global pricing. They are demanding that companies deal with them using the distribution channels they choose (manufacturer-direct and through dealers and retailers).

They are transforming industries – witness the impact of Napster on the music industry, where customers are demanding the ability to download digital music, to mix and match their own compilations, and to be able to share them with friends and other interested listeners around the world. Most important: customer relationships now count in a way that they have never counted before. Companies' values will increasingly be based on the value of their customer franchise, the lifetime customer value of their present and future customers.

So the customer is king, queen, and dictator on the Internet. But how is that different from what you've said before?

My previous book had a target audience of business executives and technology managers. My goal was to give them a common language and a common set of best practices they could use in forging their e-commerce strategies. Back in 1998, when *Customers.com* was published, many people were very confused about how to forge the right strategy for the Internet. What I saw, at the time, was that a simple strategy was the key to success: you use the net to make it easy for your customers to do business with you. Of course, it was simple to say, but hard to do. *The Customer Revolution* is written for the same audience but also for investors who want to understand the source of value in the new economy. In the last book, I kept the information technology discussions separate so that business people could skip over them. In this book, technology is just woven into the fabric of the stories. It's no longer separate.

Does that reflect changes in the business world?

Business executives have a much deeper understanding of information technology today than they did three years ago. The key messages in this book are that the companies that will win in the customer economy are already managing their companies by and for customer value. They use customer lifetime value as a strategic management tool, not just as a marketing discipline. And they measure what matters to customers in near real time.

These companies focus on the branded customer experience – on the feelings that customers have when they interact with your products and your brand across interaction touchpoints (Web, e-mail, phone, face to face) and across distribution channels (retail, dealers, agents, brokers). To win in the customer economy you need to build and sustain an exquisite branded experience and to measure and monitor what matters to customers. That's new.

What does that mean for the way companies are managed?

Notice that the companies that are the most successful have a high-level executive who is responsible for the total customer experience across product lines and distribution channels. For example, Hewlett-Packard, under Carly Fiorina, now has two large customer enterprises – one for consumers and one for business customers. Each one has a president. And reporting directly to that president is a VP of total customer

To win in the customer economy you need to build and sustain an exquisite branded experience and to measure and monitor what matters to customers. That's new

experience. This person is responsible for setting the customer experience metrics for the entire enterprise, for measuring and constantly improving the customer experience, and has the purview and the power to make policy and pricing decisions. This VP also sets the goals against which all of HP's executives are compensated.

In the customer economy, your executives' and employees' performance-based pay is based on customer metrics – how you're doing in meeting customer satisfaction and customer loyalty goals.

Give us an idea of the kinds of things you'd want companies to measure.

There are many possible measures, of course, but I'd start with making sure that managers set goals and measure how the company is doing with growth in number of active customers, growth in customers' commitments to you, customer retention, customers' propensity to defect, customer referrals, customer acquisition costs, and share of customers' wallets.

Would these measures be top secret, known by only a few on the management team?

No! I'd have these measures widely known. Expose them to your employees and partners, not just to your top management team. In fact, you must ensure that your employees and partners see these metrics and are committed to the importance of improving them for the profitability of your business.

You argue that investors should also pay more attention to customer metrics as an indicator of future profitability. But do you think that the investment community is ready to listen to your message?

At a subliminal level, investors already have a good understanding about the relationship between future earnings and customer satisfaction. Often that is based on the gut instinct that how a company treats its customers is important to future value. In a sense, then, the value of customer franchises is already factored into investment decisions. In the next few years, that will become much more explicit.

I think the investment community is much more aware now of which companies are really good at collecting customer metrics. What I'm saying is that it is time to take this to the next level. If customer satisfaction is a good lead indicator of profitability, which it is, then analysts should be tracking it too. If a company's projected value is based on the lifetime value of its present and future customers, it follows that investment decisions should take account of these metrics.

If customer satisfaction is a good lead indicator of profitability, which it is, then analysts should be tracking it too

Do you see customer metrics becoming a key criterion for investment decisions?

By 2005, I predict that most companies will be disclosing some basic customer satisfaction metrics on a quarterly basis. The investment community will demand this information. From there I would expect them to move to publishing monthly reports. Ultimately, as companies become more and more sophisticated in measuring customer metrics, this information could be made available in something approaching real time, just as financial information and share prices are at present.

You sound sure of this.

Every industry is under siege by its customers. To reflect again on Napster, what happened there was not an isolated experience. There are "renegade" customers in every industry, and they're creating demands that the major industry players simply won't be able to ignore. Although Napster hit a legal brick wall, there are many other Napster substitutes springing up, which proves, doesn't it, that the Napster revolt wasn't about copyright infringement; it was about letting customers have it *their* way. So I say, firmly, that what happened in the music industry will happen in your industry, sooner or later. It's a radical movement. Customers are wresting control away from suppliers, and customers are dictating the new business practices for the digital age. With this enormous pressure being exerted by customers in the future, it makes sense that companies ahead of the curve on this will make customer metrics key for all their decisions.

What is the key question you ask when you go into a company?

Who/which top executive is responsible for the quality of the total customer experience across product lines, distribution channels, and interaction touchpoints?

What distinguishes a lasting management idea from a fad?

Does it have "soul"? Many fads are "quick hits" with a focus on bottom-line impact or on increasing stock price. A truly lasting management idea delivers such fundamental benefits to *everyone* involved that it improves the quality of the people's lives.

If you had one question and one piece of advice for the managers of the world, what would they be?

Question: How do your company's products and services improve the quality of people's lives? Advice: focus on improving the quality of the experience that customers have every time they interact with your company's brand, through your products, your people, your services, your interaction touchpoints (phone, Web, e-mail, face to face), and your distribution partners.

[adrian slywotzky]

e-strategist

a business mind who sees the e-world changing business for ever

Adrian Slywotzky (born 1951) has been involved in a string of truly *avant garde* business books. Starting with *Value Migration* (1996, HBS Press) in the mid-1990s, Slywotzky then co-authored *The Profit Zone* (1998, Times Books) and *Profit Patterns* (1999, Random House). He most recently co-authored *How Digital Is Your Business?* (2000, Crown). Based on these provocative books, one publication called him one of the "strategists of the century," while yet another hailed him as "guru of the new economy."

Slywotzky is a vice president and member of the board of directors of Mercer Management Consulting, Inc., a global strategy consulting firm that focusses on the development of strategies for growth in changing markets. He is also responsible for the development of the firm's intellectual property.

Both a Harvard B-school and law school graduate, he is a frequent speaker on the changing face of business strategy; he presents at major corporate meetings as well as at major conferences (such as The World Economic Forum at Davos). In his writings and presentations, Slywotzky tests the common wisdom about how companies should strategize and how they can most effectively bring a strategy to

life. For more about him, go to *http://www.mercermc.com/Books/TheProfitZone/AdrianSlywotzky.html*.

In this interview, Slywotzky shares his thoughts about how the e-world will fundamentally change the business context of those who are strategically savvy.

Is the emerging impact of e-business going to change companies significantly?

I'm convinced that a massive shift to digital business worldwide is only a few years off. A few companies (only a few!) are already leading the way in the US. For some time, I've been looking more closely at how this phenomenon is happening in both Europe and Asia.

Everyone I've mentioned this to said that finding digital business models in Europe and Asia would be a real challenge – and, of course, they have all been wrong. There are some very smart companies that are mobilizing in a digital-smart way. I have not seen any companies that are ahead of the few in the US which are digital pioneers, but what I am seeing is an array of companies that understand the vast potential here.

The vast potential?

Given the right business strategy and the prospect of success being hinged to being digital, a lot of European and Asian companies completely understand that they can act like the investor who thinks contrarian during a recession. By making themselves digital today, in a very short time they can quite possibly leapfrog the number-one players anywhere in the world.

Put another way, a company does not have to be in the US to think like Amazon.com did a few years ago. You're going to see that kind of leapfrogging happening with European and Asian enterprises, and I'm watching these far-sighted companies to see just how they're going to make it happen.

Some big e-businesses are starting to sag. Maybe being digital isn't the big thing we all anticipated.

You have to separate the imaginary dot.com businesses from the real businesses that have used digital technology to build a better business model. When I mention the few companies at the forefront right now, I'd have to put Dell, Cisco, and Schwab on that list. These are companies that are showing the rest of the world how to move from a conventional business model to a digital one – and that you can make the move and have business performance and profit margins and growth rates a full ten points higher than competitors.

But having a truly new business model, fully and well executed, is rare. Only a handful of companies have done that. Those early mythic e-businesses – e-Bay, AOL, and Yahoo – seem to be looking more solid every day. And very soon we'll find out if another mythic company, Amazon.com, can go beyond its early success, develop a sustainable business model, and do it before it runs out of time.

Unfortunately, when a downturn hits, most managers resort to 10 percent across-the-board cuts

The 1990s were so good for so many companies, digital or not. Do you think that most managers are able to deal with a downturn in business?

Most are not. Most managers today do not remember prior downturns; they certainly may not have learned very much about how a downturn can be a huge opportunity if they work to prepare the company to improve its relative position in their industry. Unfortunately, when a downturn hits, most managers resort to 10 percent across-the-board cuts. What they should be doing is investing *more* in areas that are critical to them, whether that be customer relations or creating a digital presence in the marketplace.

During the big downturn in 1991, Intel invested heavily on a number of fronts. One of them was advertising. With "Intel Inside" becoming a well-known message during that period, Intel bounced back much more strongly when the recession changed to more bullish times.

A lot of executives are too timid to get online. Do you see that?

Sure. Lots of execs harbor e-fears. However, I always point out to these men and women that they are simply six hours away from being comfortable and becoming ready to take advantage of the Internet. A lot of companies should take a lesson from Jack Welch and what he did at GE: get some e-savvy 25-year-olds and link them, for only an hour a week, with top executives to teach them how to do basic stuff – open a stock portfolio in Schwab, design your own customized computer system on Dell, and so forth. Executives are amazed what happens when they spend just 60 minutes a week for six weeks. They find out first hand what the Internet is good for and what it's not good for.

How many execs would you say are competent on a computer?

In the technology sector, 90 percent. In other fields, 30 percent.

Okay, how many customers are digital ready?

Oh, it's still a small percentage. But that's not the point. The point is that the customer base is moving rapidly in this direction, and in five years or less the digital marketplace will be absolutely huge. I keep asking: Are you and your business digital enough to compete?

What about the executive who still demurs, who orders his subordinate to get online and get back to him with whatever's important?

My best story on this involves Lorenzo Zambrano at CEMEX. Back in 1992, he started communicating with his top management team via e-mail. A lot of his top managers balked. They said, "Lorenzo, why are you doing this? You have two secretaries!" He shot back, "You're missing the point!"

So moving a business into the digital age is a lot more than hiring a crew to build your company a great Web site and then operating your business as you did in the 1980s?

The reason that the digital challenge is greater than the quality movement, or even reengineering, is that strategy absolutely must come first and being digital is second. You have to ask these questions: What is the most important direction for my business? And *then* ask, What's the right approach? And finally, What part of my direction needs to be digital? Put

another way, you have to ask what technology can do for me and my company given my customer, business, industry, and marketplace.

Strategy absolutely must come first. Get that wrong, and you'll find that becoming more digital will only move you in the wrong direction faster. You have to reinvent your business model first and then digitize.

Do you spend a lot of time online?

I spend most of my time with my customers talking about strategy. But yes, I do spend time online, of course.

And how much has being online been personally rewarding to you? Do you enjoy it?

Yes, I really do. When you get online and find an enterprise that's using digital technology in just the right way, it's like discovering how business should always have been done. Why should anyone go to a store

Strategy absolutely must come first

and buy predesigned objects in predetermined packages at preset prices?

The Internet allows me, a customer, to design and acquire *exactly* what I want, without being forced to buy stuff I don't want that's attached to stuff I do want. And I can make a transaction and get it right in five minutes rather than running around day and night for days. As more companies start to understand the advantages of being digital, it's going to be a better world and a much more effective marketplace.

[don tapscott]

e-community builder

a business mind who stresses media as much as management

Don Tapscott (born 1947, in Canada) was named "one of the most influential media authorities since Marshall McLuhan" by *The Washington Technology Report.* He is an internationally sought-after authority and speaker on the impact of information and communication technologies on business, education, and society.

The former chairman of Itemus, a leading architect of next-generation Internet strategies, solutions, and software for Global 2000 organizations, Tapscott is a keen observer and reporter of the rapid technological, cultural, and economic transformations being brought about by the Internet.

His first book, *Paradigm Shift: The New Promise of Information Technology* (1992, McGraw Hill), was the first to describe the fundamental change in computing from host-based systems for controlling costs to networks for transforming business models and strategy *Growing Up Digital: The Rise of the Net Generation* (1999, McGraw Hill) won the first Amazon.com Bestseller Award. His latest book, co-authored with David Ticoll and Alex Lowy, is *Digital Capital: Harnessing the Power of Business Webs* (2000, HBS Press), a book that *BusinessWeek* called "pure enlightenment." More about Tapscott can be found at *http://www.dontapscott.com.*

In this interview, Tapscott explains how the e-world is, in many ways, a community.

Are we living in the technological and social revolution that Alvin Toffler predicted decades ago?

Toffler and other writers discussed the emergence of an information society, and it is certainly true that a new community is replacing the old capitalist industrial order that, with its own emergence, replaced the feudal, agrarian wave. Historically, we moved from an age based on steel, cars, and roads to a new age supported by computers and nets. This paradigm shift has implications for business, economics, and all other facets of society.

What are some significant business consequences?

What we are seeing is a fundamental change in the rules of success that govern both business and social development: the rise of business communities. A new sector is emerging from the convergence of the three Cs – computing, communication, and content. This triangle, defined in a strict sense, represents more than 10 percent of the gross national product in the United States. At the end of 1996, this sector was worth $1 trillion, divided as follows: 44 percent computing, 28 percent communications, and another 28 percent content. By 2005, it will have grown to an industry of $1.47 trillion, a growth of almost 50 percent.

Convergence, or business communities, is the new common denominator of economics?

Yes. We now see a fundamentally new organizational form taking shape, made up of fluid congregations of businesses – sometimes highly structured, sometimes amorphous – that come together on the Internet to create value for customers and wealth for their shareholders. This business web (b-web) can be described as a universal business platform made up of a distinct system of suppliers, distributors, commerce services providers, infrastructure providers, and customers.

If what you say comes true, this new organizational form will wield incredible influence.

The new media industry already has transformed into the base of all other sectors. As electric energy and the development of roads made possible the infrastructure of the industrial economy, the information highway – a result of convergence – has become the basis of the new economy. These new media are already changing the arts, how science is conducted, and education. They are on the verge of transforming the company and even society as we know it, changing the very nature of business, how we work, have fun, and probably, the way we think.

Wasn't reengineering also about changing the basic fabric of the organization?

In spite of the eloquent declarations by reengineering advocates about the improvements in service to the client, the real objective of many

But even if downsizing is good in certain situations, it is not a good strategy for the future

reengineering initiatives is to mold the processes and reduce cost, mainly in relation to people. Obviously, companies need to control or reduce their costs. No doubt the old processes of the old economy are an obstacle to competitiveness. But even if downsizing is good in certain situations, it is not a good strategy for the future. The transformation of the model of the firm has to go beyond that neutron bomb. The success of the new economy requires the invention of new processes of business, new businesses, new industries, and new clients.

Business webs, then, are a direct challenge to organizing as we've grown to understand it.

The business web is the first significant challenge to the traditional hierarchically and functionally based organization. The corporation is dead; long live the b-web. While management fads have been regarded as good medicine, the corporation largely remained sacrosanct and unchanged. The business web provides a new model for the corporation. It is not simply another take on the virtual organization, which was more of a transactional system than a true business system. Initiatives such as outsourcing, virtual organizations, eco-nets, and keritsu are interpretations of business webs – variations on a theme but lacking a grasp of the bigger organizational picture.

Are electronic communities and b-webs the future of a "free" market?

These communities are electronic networks of producers, retailers, commercial go-betweens, clients, and even competitors. Their mission is simple: collectively producing products and services through a narrow exchange of information, knowledge, and payments purely online. These communities are already rebuilding whole industries and, in certain economic areas, modifying the concept of company as

we know it. Before, the model was of a self-sufficient company, owning internally all the value chain for its business.

For example?

There is a big real estate market in Tokyo. This opportunity is being explored by clusters of net businesses. Where? On the other side of the Pacific. One is in Calgary (Canada) and another in San Francisco. They are companies with timber and domestic appliances, architects, and builders. It's called "The Internetworked Building Group." The Japanese client chooses the floors, the number of bedrooms, and other details. When the drawing is ready, he can walk through the virtual house on the screen and calculate in real time the final cost. This project is then passed on to other partners of the cluster which start producing the structure in different places where there are the necessary competencies and raw material. Three weeks later, the house is in a container and on the way to Tokyo to be assembled. Without the net it would take months to build the house.

Thus your concept of "collaborative advantage"?

First, competitive advantage is still important. However, it can be frequently reached through cooperation with competitors. That is the case of THISCO (The Hotel Industry Switch Company), formed by the world's biggest hotel groups. They cooperate to give common services and have a common reservation system. This has obvious benefits for all of them and for the hotel business as a whole.

In this model of the new organizational form, is there room for middle management?

The functions and people that are positioned in the middle will have to go up in the value chain. Otherwise they will lose their place. Here are some examples: musicians and their producers will no longer need the record labels, shops, or broadcasting companies when their music enters a net database; farmers will no longer need wholesalers and supermarkets when the consumer shops weekly from home; and hotels will say goodbye to travel agents for reservations.

The majority of business people tremble just hearing the theoretical boldness of such assertions.

We're not talking theory here, we're talking practice. New tool-based teamwork, sharing of knowledge, and globalization are growing daily. Those activities and behaviors are absolutely natural to a new, emerging workforce – a workforce that will not tolerate the hierarchy of the classical business model, not even of the traditional family. It will be very interesting, in the coming years, to see what will happen in those companies and families that refuse a more open communication.

New tool-based teamwork, sharing of knowledge, and globalization are growing daily

What impacts might we expect to see when the net generation joins the workforce?

When that generation comes to adulthood, it will become a very powerful tool for change in organizations, markets, and society. In a certain sense, it has already begun to happen. Children and youngsters lucky enough to have grown up "digitally" are innovators, well taught in the new media, strongly independent, and globally oriented. They're already changing schools, universities, and consumer markets. When they come into the companies, they will bring a new working culture.

One of your cultural predictions has been a rebirth of community spirit.

The days of children sitting passively in front of the television are dying rapidly. The TV is dead and that's it. It is being eaten by the Web. The TV sets in the future won't be more than an additional Web site. Same with the personal computer as a site for singular, passive play. Personal computing is more and more "interpersonal" – people use the computers to relate to others online. The PC became a means of communication.

Kids are better at this than adults?

For kids, this is natural; for adults, it is not. The kids get on that computer and create those communities, share information, expect to be heard and understood. In return, they listen to others as information comes in and others share what they understand. For kids, computers are for normal people, not for closed communities of technological people or computer addicts.

[alvin toffler]

super futurist

a business mind who has been predictably right about what's coming

Alvin Toffler (born 1928) is quite probably the most famous futurist alive. *Time* magazine described him as the person "who set the standard by which all subsequent would-be futurists have been measured." It would be difficult to name another author who has been more influential in creating a dialogue on what will happen in society in the future.

Toffler's books are all classics which have made an impact. *Future Shock, The Third Wave* (1970, Bodley Head), and *Creating a New Civilization* (1995, Turner Publishing) added memorable words and phrases to our language, from "future shock" and "electronic cottage" to "demassification" and "overchoice." These concepts, and their impact on business, are still being studied and widely debated.

The influence of Toffler's ideas have been cited from the White House to the Kremlin, as world governments seek his counsel on how to prepare for the future. Ted Turner publicly credited Toffler with inspiring him to launch the Cable News Network.

Toffler's many awards include the McKinsey Foundation Book Award for Contributions to Management Literature, and France's prestigious Prix du Meilleur Livre Etranger. Moreover, he has been elected a fellow of the American Association for the Advancement of Science. He has taught at Cornell University and the New School

for Social Research, and has served as a White House correspondent, an editor for *Fortune* magazine, and a business consultant. More information about this progressive thinker can be found at *http://www.toffler.com*.

In this interview, Toffler talks about history and the future, and what they mean to the marketplace.

In your work you've created a vocabulary for reconceptualizing history.

My starting point has always been "change." Things change, and they need to change, and change is driven by technology and knowledge. But change comes at a cost, sometimes a very high cost. The master conflict of the 21st century will not be between cultures but between the three super civilizations – between agrarianism, industrialism, and post-industrialism. The emerging third-wave civilization is going to collide head-on with the old first and second civilizations. One of the things we ought to learn from history is that when waves of change collide, they create countercurrents. When the first and the second wave collided, we had civil wars, upheavals, political revolutions, forced migrations. Humanity faces a quantum leap forward. It faces the deepest social upheaval and creative restructuring of all time. Without clearly recognizing it, we are engaged in building a remarkable new civilization from the ground up. This is the meaning of the third wave.

Such predictions imply immense changes for businesses.

Of course. The essence of second-wave manufacture was the long "run" of millions of identical, standardized products. By contrast, the essence of third-wave manufacture is the short run of partially or completely customized products. The organization of the future will be concerned with environmental stewardship, social accountability, knowledge management, the integration of business and governmental agencies, and ethics on a much larger scale than ever before.

Global change and instability has been a constant theme in your work. What change issue is foremost in your mind right now?

I've been concentrating on the problem of social and cultural conditions for the creation of wealth in modern times. These processes are complex, far more so than was assumed by Westerners, for example, when they got to the USSR with their plans for implementing a capitalistic market. They discovered that basic conditions were lacking, such as the requisite legal system. And the monster they created has nothing to do with what they thought they were "transplanting." In fact, in Eastern Europe the most massive transitions of the system are occurring right now, the most complex problems of the planet for years to come.

Are you optimistic?

It's not easy to be optimistic. Russia is like a boiling pan – emerging fascism, tactical nuclear weapons at hand, wild capitalism – all the ingredients necessary to explode at one point or another. In China, however, a revolution is at hand that runs deeper than Mao Tse-tung's Cultural Revolution, and it is one that Chinese leaders want to accomplish with stability. It is a revolutionary effort to free people from poverty. Given the scope of the problem it will be amazing if they succeed. But if Asia can free 1 billion people from poverty, it will be something unseen in world history.

So deep down, you're hopeful about Asia?

Contrary to what is often said these days, I don't think that Asia is fin-ished. In my books I anticipated a lot of turbulence and warned that continuous economic growth could stop. Of course, nobody knows the future, but I'm hopeful that Asia will come back. There is a tremendous energy in its "basement" – human resources are still there. There is a hard core that wasn't liquidated, which is still working for the future. It has been an uphill battle, made worse by short-sighted assistance from sources like the International Monetary Fund (IMF). Sincerely, I think the IMF has its hands covered with blood in Asia. It didn't understand a thing about what was going on there.

What about Europe?

I would also like to know what will happen. After the Second World War, the purpose of integration was political. However, according to my

Of course, nobody knows the future, but I'm hopeful that Asia will come back

terminology, it didn't come rightfully with a dive into the third wave. Europe still hasn't discovered it, it's true, after 50 years. If you talk to me about the European brands of the third wave, I can find only one exception – software company SAP AG. The rest, I'm sorry to say, is dead and more than dead. Europe's political and even business community, as hard as it is to hear, still lives essentially in the past. The implicit strategy of its governments is still this: feed the first wave, with the agriculture lobby increasing its weight; sustain the second wave, so that non-competitive companies survive; and ignore, as a whole, the entrepreneurs of the third wave.

What seems to be the problem?

What can I say to you? Politically, I think a great mistake was made in Europe. The lucid critics of the left and central wing were put aside. The only critical presence given a voice – and it is even more old-fashioned than the left – is from the extremists of the right wing, which is terrible. European politicians are still dazzled with the euro, but after the first two or three years they'll change. I even think that some European politicians are already aware of the problems. They understand what is going on, but they can't take the necessary steps because clients don't let them. The third wave means change, deep change, and a lot of people with power and privileges don't want it.

Will the Internet bring us any more "future shocks"?

Let's see, I was among the handful of maybe 700 who, in the 1970s, already used that communication tool to develop a tremendous cooperative work. We were a very small community at the time. Then, at the end of the 1980s, the media discovered the Internet. The idea that was transmitted, too often from that point of view, was that previously there was nothing, that the net came out of the blue. Obviously it was not like that. From the beginning we were convinced that it was something that would completely revolutionize institutions, like the family, finance, commerce, the media. Now saying this is just a cliché. I think that the net will not be a revolution for work and commerce only. The home, our home, the place we live, is an emerging place. It is as if there was a return, a dialectic one, to the pre-industrial phase.

How about the "new economy"? Real, or is it also hype journalism and marketing?

There has been a caricatured debate on the problem. On one side there are the "purists" saying there is nothing new, and that what is going on with the "hi-tech" stock is unjustified madness. On the other there are the defenders of the new economy, tending to defend a naive optimism about continuous, neverending growth. I think both sides are wrong. There certainly is a new economy! But it's naive to think about a neverending stability, when reality is pure turbulence. The essential question is how to develop a strategy based on knowledge – a national strategy. And that is where the efforts of the debate should concentrate.

What do you mean by a national strategy based on knowledge?

What is now needed is that countries think, on a national level, about strategies of this kind. For me, there are two fundamental stepping-stones for such a strategy: a better education, and a good electronic infrastructure. We have an absolute need of new ways of teaching, in which media themselves have to be involved, computers, shared knowledge, families, teachers, consultants, etc. I'm talking about an extraordinary level of involvement, such as the TV Globo project as part of the "500 Years of the Discovery of Brazil" observance. This is an educational project, primarily for young Brazilians. National strategies involving multiple constituencies aimed at educating masses of people will be one of the great – and most crucial – challenges of the future.

[fons trompenaars]

cultural reconciler

a business mind who melds cultures into progress

Fons Trompenaars (born 1953, in The Netherlands) is founder of Trompenaars Hampden-Turner, an Amsterdam-based consultancy on cross-cultural management issues. Trompenaars continues the groundbreaking work he began as a doctoral student at the Wharton School.

He and Charles Hampden-Turner also wrote *The Seven Cultures of Capitalism: Value Systems for Creating Wealth in the United States, Japan, Germany, France, Britain, Sweden, and the Netherlands* (1994, Piatkus), and most recently *21 Leaders for the 21st Century* (2001, John Wiley), and *Building Cross-Cultural Competence* (2000, John Wiley). His book *Riding the Waves of Culture: Understanding Cultural Diversity in Business* (1993, Nicholas Brealey) builds on his experience with Royal Dutch Shell (1981–9) for which he worked in nine countries.

Trompenaars has consulted to many multinational companies ranging from Goldman Sachs to Motorola to Dow Chemicals, with the aim of "recognizing, respecting, and reconciling cultural differences." Many of the training programs delivered by the consultancy focus on the company's "Seven Dimensions of Culture Model." For more information, connect to *http://www.thtconsulting.com/*.

In this interview, Trompenaars focusses on how to deal with the complexities of culture, especially in thinking about strategies.

You speak frequently about "cultural reconciliation." What does this mean?

Simply put, it refers to the necessity of reconciling the host of cultural differences between employees, or, for that matter, citizens of a country. Reconciled cultures have created a culture of their own by enriching the cultures of the partners involved. Organizations and societies that can reconcile cultural differences better are better at creating wealth. It's as simple as that.

That sounds reasonable. Why is it so difficult to accomplish?

Culture is a series of rules and methods that a society has evolved to deal with the recurring problems it faces. They have become so basic that, like breathing, we no longer think about how we approach or resolve them. Every country and every organization faces dilemmas in relationships with people, dilemmas in relationship to time, and dilemmas in relationships between people and the natural environment. Mix and match people from different cultures, who interpret such issues diversely, and you have organizational chaos that has to be managed differently than other organization issues.

Cultural mixing is an everyday feature of organizational life, especially in these times of huge corporate acquisitions, mergers, and alliances. Relational aspects like cultural differences and lack of trust are responsible for 70 percent of alliance failures. This is even more striking when we realize that building trust is a cultural challenge in itself. Lack of trust is often caused by different views of what constitutes a trust-

worthy partner. In addition, intercultural alliances involve differences in corporate cultures as well as national cultures. Perceptions of these, as well as of more or less "objective" cultural variations, can lead to big problems.

Is there a way to predict typical sorts of clashes that might arise in a large alliance or merger?

There are seven continua that characterize the predictable dilemmas in need of reconciliation. Universalism-particularism is the battle over standardized rules versus flexibility; Individualism-communitarianism is the question of what the organization most promotes: individualism or group cohesiveness; neutral-affective is the question of emotional control versus emotional display; specific-diffuse asks how personally involved in business the employee is; achievement-ascription is the organization's stance on status based on merit as opposed to other factors, such as age or family background; sequential-synchronic refers to

Lack of trust is often caused by different views of what constitutes a trustworthy partner

time orientation – whether employees deal with time (and projects) sequentially or in parallel, juggling multiple projects simultaneously; and internal-external control is a question of motivation – whether it tends to come from within or outside of the person.

In the case of a merger or alliance, when faced with cultural differences, how should the organizations respond?

One effective approach is to compare the two profiles to identify where the major differences originate. In practice, the major origin of cultural differences between your organization and the new partner may lie in the most dominant one or two cultural dimensions. By reconciling the dilemmas deriving from the differences on the dimensions, organizations can begin to reconcile their cultural orientations.

Your ideas suggest a radical redesign of the manager's job, especially international managers.

Absolutely! How international managers reconcile differences is the very essence of their job. The international manager needs to go beyond awareness of cultural differences. He or she needs to respect these differences and take advantage of diversity through reconciling cross-cultural dilemmas.

For example?

Consider the fundamental differences between the universalist and the particularist. Universalists (including Americans, Canadians, Australians, and the Swiss) advocate "one best way," a set of rules that applies in any setting. Particularists (South Koreans, Chinese, and Malaysians) focus on the peculiar nature of any given situation. Uni-

versalists doing business with particularists should, for example, be prepared for meandering or irrelevancies that do not seem to be going anywhere. Moreover, they should not take "get to know you chatter" as small talk – it is important to particularists. Particularists doing business with universalists should be prepared for straightforward, no-nonsense, rational, and professional arguments and presentations. We need a certain amount of humility and a sense of humor to discover cultures other than our own, a readiness to enter a room in the dark and stumble over unfamiliar furniture until the pain in our shins reminds us of where things are. Most managers, it seems, are more intent on protecting their shins than blundering through darkened rooms.

Do any success stories come to mind?

Executives like Jim Morgan of Applied Materials, Karel Vuursteen from Heineken, Acer's Stan Shih, Anders Knutsen of Bang and Olufsen, and Club Med's Philippe Bourguignon have typically resolved three or more of these dilemmas. A great example is McDonald's. Its recent success has been built through globalizing local learning. During the Asian crisis it found it couldn't import potatoes into Malaysia so it reintroduced rice onto the menu. This was a great success so it tried it out elsewhere in the world. It worked.

All of your examples are men.

We did have difficulty finding women leaders for the leadership book. First of all, there aren't that many female senior executives, and the first 25 we approached to be interviewed all said they were too busy. Men said the same but usually relented. The women did not. Our conclusion is that they are less vain. Too bad because they seem to be better reconcilers than men.

How can an alliance predict intercultural dilemmas?

We have developed a methodology that we call cultural due diligence. This provides an operational framework intended to be facilitated by the HR directorate to make these cultural differences tangible so that their consequences can be made explicit and thereby reconciled to ensure benefit delivery. It is based on the three Rs: recognition, respect, and reconciliation.

Recognition, respect, and reconciliation refer, essentially, to what?

The first task for human resources is to help all players recognize that there are cultural differences, their importance, and how they impact organizational life. The second task is to demonstrate to organizational members that different cultural orientations and views of the world are not right or wrong – they are just different. And the third task is to

In our experience HR professionals can play a crucial role in the facilitation of a successful reconciliation of cultures

demonstrate the growing conviction that wealth is created in alliances (including mergers and acquisitions) by reconciling values. This is a new contribution to the debate on alliances and mergers in business. Cultural due diligence is the means to bring about reconciliation of these seemingly opposing views.

The human resources professional, then, plays a central role in the success of any corporate alliance?

It is a prerequisite that HR professionals are engaged in the integration process as early as possible. Unfortunately, in many situations their expected contribution often is limited to developing an early retirement scheme for those people who become redundant because of the expected economies of scale of the integration. In our experience HR professionals can play a crucial role in the facilitation of a successful reconciliation of cultures. They need to become "culture coaches" facilitating the basic processes of post- and pre-merger integration. They are in the best position in the organization to link HR activities to the inherent and overt strategy of the alliance or merger.

For the manager, then, cultural due diligence accomplishes what?

This approach will inform managers how to guide the social side of alliances of any kind. It has a logic that integrates differences. It is a series of behaviors that enables effective interaction with those of contrasting value systems. It reveals a propensity to share understanding of others' positions in the expectation of reciprocity and requires a new way of thinking that is initially difficult for Westerners. Put differently, international success in alliances depends upon discovering special veins of excellence within different cultures. Just because people speak English does not mean they think alike. That no two cultures are the same is what brings richness and complexity to multinationalism. Cultural due diligence gives the manager that understanding. And with it, the manager stands a reasonable chance of reconciling the cultural dilemmas that so often derail the best-laid alliance plans.

[bruce tulgan]

talent champion

a business mind attuned to workplace demographics – and attitudes

Bruce Tulgan (born 1967) is renowned for the influential book *Managing Generation X* (1996, Capstone), which distilled the work ethic of the post-baby boomer generation and alerted corporations to a major shift in employee attitudes. He has addressed thousands of managers on the subject and has even been called "the new Tom Peters."

Tulgan's career reflects his GenX origins. In 1993, he left a successful career with a Wall Street law firm to found RainmakerThinking, a New Haven, Connecticut, company that focusses on new management practices for the new economy through its ongoing research into the working lives of those born after 1963 (which now extends to Generation Y, those born between 1978 and 1984).

A long-standing champion of "free agency," Tulgan has taught at the graduate level and remains a prolific writer of articles and books. His new book, *Winning the Talent Wars* (2000, W.W. Norton), takes aim at the staffing crisis facing the business world. An attorney who has practiced law, and a fourth-degree black belt in Okinawan karate, Tulgan has a fascinating business mind. Tulgan's company's website tells more about him, at *http://www.rainmakerthinking.com*.

What are the primary forces driving the battle for talent?

I argue that the talent wars are not growing out of a short-term "hot" economy but rather out of the fundamental paradigm shift in the employer–employee relationship. From the old slow-moving, rigid, pay-your-dues-and-climb-the-ladder model to the new fast-moving, increasingly efficient free market for talent. Employing people in the new economy requires a whole new approach to management and a whole new set of management practices.

Characterize these changes you refer to in the employer–employee relationship.

We are living through the most profound changes in the economy since the Industrial Revolution. Technology, globalization, and the accelerating pace of change have yielded chaotic markets, fierce competition, and unpredictable staffing requirements. Business leaders and managers began responding to these factors by seeking much greater organizational flexibility. Reengineering increased speed and efficiency with improved systems and technology. Companies in every industry have redesigned almost everything about the way work gets done in an effort to improve flexibility, efficiency, and effectiveness.

Workplaces became more adaptable?

The changes in the economy have been freeing work from the confines of the old-fashioned "job" with its rigid features: employees going every day to the same organization in the same building during the same hours to do the same tasks and responsibilities in the same position in the same chain of command, paying their dues and climbing the ladder. Now, the rule of thumb is that you get the work done, whenever you can, wherever you can, however you can, whatever the work

may be on any given day. As a result, business organizations have become more nimble than ever before and are now much better able to compete in today's high-tech, fast-paced, knowledge-driven, global economy. But, in the process, the nature of work has been fundamentally reshaped and the relationship between employers and employees radically altered for ever. In the new economy, the old-fashioned model of work is all but gone.

And replaced with what?

The new economy forced change onto the organizational landscape. But when business leaders responded by killing the old model of success – the dues-paying career path defined by long-term employment in one company and corporate loyalty – very few predicted that, in response, the workers with the most marketable skills, the people consistently in greatest demand, would discover that they could do better

People, especially the best educated and most skilled, increasingly see themselves as sole proprietors of their skills and abilities – free agents

fending for themselves than they ever had by following the old-fashioned career path. But that's exactly what happened, and a whole new career path emerged: the path of free agency.

Workers as free agents?

People, especially the best educated and most skilled, increasingly see themselves as sole proprietors of their skills and abilities – free agents. These free agents think of their employers as "clients," often juggling several at once. They seem to move seamlessly from one new opportunity to the next, soaking up training resources, building relationships with decision makers, and collecting proof of their ability to add value, and cash out their career investments on a regular basis so they can reassess and renegotiate.

With so much moving around, how does this free agent/employee measure success?

To the free agent, success is not defined by where they stand in relation to the hierarchy of a particular organization. What matters is their ability to add value and to sell that value on the open market. Every untapped resource is waiting to be mined. Every unmet need is an opportunity to add value. Every person is a potential customer. This is not a group to be underestimated. They are adaptable, independent, techno-literate, information savvy, and entrepreneurial. They are, in short, what most organizations need.

Is this mindset widespread?

Today, free agency is sweeping across the workforce like wildfire. More and more people are coming to realize that to keep doing what they know how to do well and earn money doing it, they don't necessarily need a permanent job, or even a job as such at all. In the new economy, the individual, not the employer, is in the driver's seat. The skills that make you valuable to an employer belong to you and nobody else. When you leave your employer, those skills and experience and ability to add value go with you. Nowadays, security comes not from stability and commitments but rather from mobility and options. And all of a sudden, fewer and fewer skilled people are clinging to their jobs and crying "don't downsize me," and the balance of power in the labor market is shifting.

What does this shift in the balance of power mean for the workplace?

The old feudal employment relationship – defined by the logic of an internal hierarchy and insulated from market forces – is dead. In a free market environment everybody gets exactly what he/she can negotiate. So everybody is going to be driving a hard bargain. The talented people who can't negotiate the best deals for themselves are going to get left behind. And employers that can't negotiate with the best talent won't be able to keep people around long enough to get all the work done. Welcome to the real new economy.

Is "free agency" the same as "Generation X"?

It's not just about Generation X any more. GenX was in the vanguard of free agency, I am now convinced, through an accident of history. Xers just happened to come into the workplace during the most profound changes in the economy since the Industrial Revolution. But the free-agent mindset is spreading across the workforce among people of all ages because the changes are not just about one generation – they are fundamental changes in the economy that are causing everybody to rethink their working lives and careers.

Given the many challenges inherent in free agency, portable talent, and the competition to attract and retain the best performers, what advice can you give to organizations?

> My advice would be to center around attending to six "best practice" concerns: staffing, training, performance management, the role of managers, rewards and incentives, and retention.

What is the essence of your staffing advice?

> In the new economy, staffing needs will be in continual flux. Employers should do three things. First, shrink your core group. Second, grow a fluid talent pool that you can draw on as needs be. Third, maintain an internal group of contributors who are not permanently assigned to any particular tasks/responsibilities, teams, locations, or schedules, who can be called on and deployed to fill in staffing gaps wherever and whenever they occur.

Training?

> Avoid the "training investment paradox" – the more companies train their employees, the more marketable those employees become and, therefore, the more likely they are to leave the organization for a better offer. Organizations need to stop training their employees for the long haul. It makes much more sense to train people only on an as-needed basis. Just-in-time training is in sync with the learning needs of individuals in today's information environment because it allows learners to select immediately the precise information they require to fill skill and knowledge gaps as they occur.

Performance management?

To bring out the very best in the very best people, managers must create clarity on an ongoing basis around three key questions: Which roles are being played by which people in pursuit of which missions? Where does each employee's responsibility begin and end? And how and for what will each contributor be held accountable?

The role of managers?

Supervisory managers in the new workplace must be performance management coaches. The most important predictor of success (productivity, morale, and duration of employment) of long-term and short-term employees, as well as of teams, is a coaching-style manager who knows how to give what we call *"fast* feedback" effectively (frequent, accurate, specific, and timely).

Long-term rewards are out. Managers need to reward desired performance consistently and with speed and creativity

Rewards and incentives?

In the just-in-time workplace, you can't expect people to wait around to be rewarded once they've delivered. Long-term rewards are out. Managers need to reward desired performance consistently and with speed and creativity. Three factors should guide rewards and incentives: control, timing, and customization. Performance should be the only lever controlling rewards – so yes, high performers do get more than low performers; rewards need to be delivered sooner rather than later; and managers need to accept that different people are motivated by very different incentives.

Retention?

The key to retention is to redefine it so that it means "access to the talent you need when you need it." With that redefinition, the way to retain talent is to stay lean and learn to thrive on short-term, flexible employment relationships with the best free-agent employees. The best people who serve you well on a consistent basis will be your new life-long employees. Retain the best people one at a time, one day at a time, on the basis of an ongoing negotiation with each individual on their own unique terms.

If you go into a company, what's the most important question you ask?

Whenever I go into an organization, I try to focus on the issues that are of greatest concern there. By talking through the issue with my key contacts – whether it is staffing strategy, organization structure, recruiting, orientation and new-employee on-boarding, training, performance management, rewards, retention, or whatever else – I want to find out what's going right and what's going wrong. Why is this issue a concern?

The problem is that often people at the top are too close to the situation to have an accurate and penetrating view. So here is the really important question: Who, on the front lines, is *not* having a problem with this issue? And then, even more important: May I talk privately with these people, one at a time?

What question would you like to ask the managers of the world?

This is the question I do often ask the managers of the world: How does it feel to be caught in the middle – between the pressures from senior executives to drive productivity and quality and the pressures from individuals you manage who are trying to get more money and more control over where, when, and how they work? And how do you manage those competing pressures in a way that balances your obligations to the company, to your employees, and to your own life and career?

[meg wheatley]

social prophet

a business mind who's prescient on trends in organizations and society

Margaret J. (Meg) Wheatley (born 1944) is president of The Berkana Institute. She is also the author of *Leadership and the New Science* (1999, Berrett Koehler), a book which, in the course of a decade, completely reframed the way people look at managing organizations. Wheatley used the principles of "chaos theory" to encourage people to think about the systems at the heart of their work lives. As a result, many adopted the same point of view to reassess how they viewed corporations and society.

Wheatley has been a public school teacher and education administrator, a Peace Corps volunteer, an associate professor of management at Brigham Young University in Utah as well as at Cambridge College in Massachusetts. As a consultant, she has worked on six continents with organizations as diverse as the US Army and the Girl Scouts. Wheatley founded The Berkana Institute in 1991 as a charitable scientific, educational, and research foundation. The institute experiments with new ideas, processes, and structures while focussing on new ways to organize in life-affirming ways.

Leadership and the New Science topped many lists as "Book of the Year" in 1992; Xerox Corporation even named it as one of the Top 10 Business Books Of All Time.

A video based on the book has been an all-time bestseller for CRM Learning. Wheatley also co-authored with Myron Kellner-Rogers *A Simpler Way* (1998, Berrett Koehler), Her newest book, due out at the end of 2001, will be titled *Turning to One Another: Simple Conversations to Restore Hope to the Future.* For more about Wheatley, log onto *http://www.margaretwheatley.com*.

In this interview, Wheatley demonstrates why her reputation as a "social prophet" is well earned as she reviews the changing nature of working, business, and society.

Your first book, *Leadership and the New Science,* completely changed how people thought about and discussed businesses and organizations. Why was it so successful?

To be sure, the book was ahead of its time. When the book first appeared, the Internet wasn't the organizing influence it is today; we were not nearly the networked world we are now. When people thought about "organizational systems" (and that was rarely), they did so in a very intellectual way. "Chaos theory" was a very abstract concept back then. However, many readers sensed, as I did, that systems, networks, interdependence, and chaos were creeping into their lives and organizations. As has been true for a long time, science and art usually lead people in describing the world that is and soon will be. I had the good fortune to be able to write about high-speed, networked, dynamic, chaotic organizational systems a few years before everyone started living in them.

The world has certainly moved ahead. Has the thinking and teaching of management done the same?

There are some very thoughtful writings in the field of management today. Whether the subject is self-organizing systems, values, or organizational flexibility and nimbleness, there are enough good studies available that – if you took them seriously – anyone could learn a very great deal about how to manage better. The trouble is, in both the corporate world and in the academic world, what I too often see is that people are "entertaining" the thoughts in the very best books, but people are not engaging progressive thinking as information that is necessary to future success, that needs to be *acted* upon.

Where, then, is the profession of management?

It's stuck. It's still captivated by old rules and old ways of organizing companies and doing business in society. If anything, the profession seems to be going backward. We know so much more today about workplaces, about marketplaces, and about human beings; yet, given today's tough economic climate, many managers are making huge leaps backwards. They are clamping down, acting reactionary, barking orders. Fear is driving managers to be "old school" in their behaviors. A young European manager recently asked me, "Isn't this a good time, during this market downturn, to be reflective and use the power of experience to build better organizations?" I told him that he was assuming that managers would set aside their fears long enough to think reflectively about how to improve their people and organization, and thus to involve everyone in the question of how to create a brighter future. Unfortunately, fear is dominating most managers' minds right now.

Is that true for business schools or corporate seminars?

I see very little progressive thinking in B-schools or corporate training programs. And we don't need time to learn new techniques right now. What we need is time to think about what we've learned from all we've been doing. Which is why I try, whenever I'm invited to speak to any

group, to raise a thoughtful conversation about what it's like right now. So many people are at, or past, the breaking point. They are feeling so incredibly trapped by organizational or business systems which demand so much – such as the now-daily demands of the stock market – that they are most often behaving without thinking, which is organizational suicide. People may be moving fast inside companies, but too often it's a scramble to disaster.

Why aren't things better?

What I hear from senior leaders is that they are under constant pressure to generate profits. There's nothing wrong with that, of course. What is wrong is that profit is becoming the *only* value around which people are organizing. The only other value I see out there is speed. Put them together, and one sees company after company trying to do just one thing: make money, fast. That combination is dangerous. We are now organizing enterprises that are destructive of the things people most

People may be moving fast inside companies, but too often it's a scramble to disaster

care about, like quality of life or good relationships with people we work with or good relationships with our family, or long-term sustainability.

What, then, do you look for when you find an organization that you consider to be progressive?

I look for three things. First, I look for a leader who's willing to admit that he or she can't run the organization alone. I look for a leader who's highly participative, because he or she knows that no one can possibly figure out a solution independently. Such leaders know that change is not going to happen unless people throughout the organization want it to happen. Second, I look for a leadership group that's willing to trust people; it's a team that believes that people in all parts of the organization can think progressively. Moreover, it's a group that is willing to bite the bullet and give people time to think. Too often, organizations moving at breakneck speed are, literally, breaking necks. So the third critical trait I look for in progressive organizations is that they have a leadership team committed to reclaiming time to think about where the organization is headed and how it needs to change.

Most businesses, however, don't act that way. Does this concern you?

I am extremely concerned about the subtle shift that's occurred in society. In fact, it's not so subtle at all. In the past, society saw businesses as part of the national economy, an essential part – a part which gave the members of the society a source of sustenance, ways to make a living. The economy supported society. Now, however, everything and everyone must justify its existence in terms of its value to the economy. What makes for a good society and a decent life does not take precedence; we have shifted so that we only care about what makes for more

and bigger businesses. We speak of a 24/7 world, but it's 24/7 in terms of conducting commerce, in terms of boosting the economy, in terms of nurturing corporations.

What's wrong with that?

What's wrong is that we find that anyone who wants time to think, time for their kids, time to grow themselves into a better human being, or even time just to explore new possibilities – such people are seen as working against the interests of the corporate world, which skews its interests primarily toward how to make money, now! And so we have the term "rat race" being revived for some very good reasons. In the US and in Japan, the lure of materialism has transformed human beings into consumers. And even when I get the chance to visit people in a country like Denmark – where many stop working at 5.30pm so they can have an evening with family and friends, where they still take whole weekends off and don't use Saturday and Sunday just to catch up on e-mails – even there, I sense that children are seeing the rest of the world through the eyes of the Internet or other media and they are buying into some very false choices. I mean, what does it say when we even have to ask the question whether we want a healthy economy or global warming? I have to challenge the mindset that asks such a silly question, as if there's a choice between those two.

Can these trends be changed?

Yes, but not by governments (which too often now exist to support global corporations, which have the real power today) nor by one person standing alone against the pressures I've outlined. Real change starts with each of us noticing how the current business environment is affecting our lives and values, personally. Then, after this kind of serious, thoughtful assessment, each person has to ask, "Is this working?"

And that question can only be answered if each person redefines "true success" according to his or her personal values. This, of course, is happening, widely. And change begins the minute one individual reaches out to other individuals and, together, this self-organizing group elects to become an agent of change. It's up to "us" now, those of us who are willing to think about what it means to be human, to be successful, to act courageously by reaching out and supporting others who want to make society and business better. No huge social program will do this. No government intervention will make change happen. We have to become the agents of change. It's up to us.

[danah zohar]

leadership physicist

a business mind shaped by physics and philosophy

Danah Zohar (born 1944) has had an unusual path to becoming a leading management guru, with an undergraduate degree from MIT in physics and philosophy and graduate work at Harvard in philosophy and psychology. While scientists have for years been measuring intelligence (IQ), neuroscientists and psychologists have for the past decade been studying emotional intelligence as a prerequisite to the effective use of IQ.

Now Zohar has added the concept of spiritual intelligence (SQ), which she says is the ultimate intelligence of the leader and the major difference between a manager and a leader. According to Zohar, SQ is the intelligence that allows leaders to see the broader picture, to ask new questions, and to innovate. In her book *ReWiring the Corporate Brain* (1997, Berrett Koehler), Zohar states that while many companies talk about change, they risk failure unless they change their basic mental, emotional, and spiritual foundations.

Zohar also collaborated on such bestselling books as *The Quantum Self* (1991, Flamingo), *The Quantum Society* (1995, Quill), and *Who's Afraid Of Schrödinger's Cat?* (1997, William Morrow) A visiting fellow at the Cranfield School of Management, Zohar also teaches in the Oxford University Strategic Leadership Program and the Leading Edge Program at Oxford Brookes University. She has spoken to many corporate, government, and industry groups throughout the world.

She is someone who loves all things Nepalese (she spends a month or two in Kathmandu every year, running workshops there for business people from the West). To learn more about Zohar, visit *http://wwwdzohar.com*.

In this interview, Zohar talks about managers and leaders in terms unique to her background and experience.

There's IQ: intelligence quotient. And then there's EQ: emotional quotient. Both have had a huge impact on people and organizations. What can SQ do that these two can't?

IQ is our rational, logical, linear intelligence. It is the intelligence with which we solve problems and with which we manipulate and control our environment. EQ, our emotional intelligence, is the intelligence with which we identify the situation we are in and behave appropriately. EQ is an *adaptive* intelligence. Both IQ and EQ work within a paradigm, within the box, within the given. We use them to play a "finite game." SQ, our need for and access to deep meaning, purpose, and values, is our *transformative* intelligence. SQ makes us ask fundamental questions, it rocks the boat and moves the boundaries. SQ allows us to understand situations deeply, to invent new categories of understanding, and to be creative. With SQ we play an "infinite game."

Some managers squirm when words like "spirit" are used in a workplace setting. Why is that?

"Spirit" is a big word with so many meanings. I use it in connection with intelligence. It makes us ask *why*. It leads us to question, to change

things, to be subversive. All that is uncomfortable stuff to your average manager. Spirit, in my sense, connotes that we ponder why we are doing what we are doing, and where it will lead. What are the alternatives? What are the costs? Business people who just want to "get on with the job" have become allergic to such reflection. It seems "soft" to them. Business is supposed to be about making money, as quickly as possible. Spirit suggests there may be more to life (and to leaders' and employees' motivations) than simply money. Perhaps what we do has to mean something, has to have some deeper purpose.

So you feel that these managers are out of touch with both their workplace and with themselves?

Yes, the pure money mongers are out of touch with their own deepest needs, and with those of their people. King Midas, who loved only gold, died of starvation when everything he owned turned to gold. We can't live in a world made of gold. Human beings are, in our most primary

Spirit suggests there may be more to life (and to leaders' and employees' motivations) than simply money

definition, creatures of meaning and value. That is what separates us from all other animals. We *have* to have meaning to function. When we have meaning, we will die for it if necessary. When we lack meaning, we become stressed and ill. Meaning gives us a time frame, a sense of higher purpose, a long-term commitment to the future. Today's business and capitalism function in a vacuum of meaning and are rushing head-long toward self-destruction.

You are able to talk science *and* management. How do you keep such different fields equally balanced in your mind?

I don't think they *are* different fields. Science has direct implications for management. Science talks about "complex-adaptive systems," and organizations potentially *are* complex-adaptive systems (holistic, self-organizing, emergent systems). Management needs new thinking; science provides it. Good science respects no paradigm; it questions all assumptions. Management could do with a good dose of such subversive thinking.

You have asserted that we live in a "spiritually dumb" culture. Why so?

The first criterion for recognizing SQ in someone is self-awareness. We live in a very self-obsessed culture, but we are very, very short on self-awareness. We are so spiritually dumb that we don't even know what we are missing. Our culture is smug, arrogant, obsessed with the immediate moment and immediate gain. Few of us, if asked, could say what it is that makes us definitively human, never mind knowing the awesome responsibility that being human entails. I think business is particularly guilty of this. Business lives for the fast buck, the consequences be damned. Business is very bad at looking inward, at evaluating itself, at asking itself uncomfortable questions. Business works in a short time frame rather than cultivating the long-term perspective. Most business practice undermines any kind of reflective thought, using only its IQ to solve immediate problems.

Given how stimulating your books are, who are the writers (or thinkers) today who challenge your assumptions and thoughts constructively?

My answer may surprise you, because apart from the complexity theorist Stuart Kauffman and good journals like *Nature* and *Scientific American,* most of my reading is outside science. I'm inspired by people like Nietzsche, Thomas Merton, Carlos Casteneda, Richard Sennett, George Steiner. I read a lot of Indian novels and also a lot of history and politics. I'm a sucker for any new book on the Third Reich, because I think we need to understand what went wrong there and why. I *never* read management books.

Do you see a "version 21" management model (a new kind of manager) emerging in the years ahead?

This is a very big question, because I think we need not only a version 21 manager (I prefer "leader") but also a version 21 human being. We need people who can think deeply, independently, and radically.

We need reflective people who know how to ask good questions. Some universal training in philosophy would go a long way! All our answers today are leading us toward disaster. We need better questions. We need people who will put service above self, people who have the courage to be spontaneous, and people who aren't afraid to get it wrong. We need people who can live at the edge of chaos, between boring predictability and disruptive innovation, between the known and the unknown. In business, we need people who can put serving fundamental values and deep purpose above the mere pursuit of short-term profit.

Shaping 21st-century people and organizations is a tall order. What's next in your path to achieve this quest?

My book in progress is to be called *Spiritual Capital*. It's about creating wealth through the pursuit of deep purpose, service, and fundamental values. Business as we know it is blinded to the future by the heedless pursuit of short-term profit amassed through short-term strategies. Today's business ethic is self-destructive and unsustainable. To survive and prosper, business needs to erase the present distinction between profit and public service. Business leaders need to become servant leaders in the most profound sense, leaders who serve the community, the planet, and life itself. Twenty years ago this would have sounded like pie-in-the-sky idealism. Today it is a matter of urgency upon which everyone's survival depends.

the-sky

More guru power to your [business-mind]

Even at the end there's more we can learn. If today's idea is tomorrow's task, then we believe there's always value to be found in getting to tomorrow's ideas first. That's why *Business Minds* is more than a book.

For who to read, what to know and where to go in the world of business, visit us at **business-minds.com**.

Here we're creating a place where you can go to connect with new business ideas as they evolve, and engage with the next generation of thought leaders.

Share the latest ideas with the people that can make you and your business more innovative and productive. Each month our e-newsletter, *Business-minds Express*, delivers an infusion of thought leadership, guru interviews, new business practice and reviews of key business resources directly to you. Subscribe for free at

www.business-minds.com/goto/newsletters

If you want to explore some of these ideas further, then at business-minds.com you'll find books by many of the gurus interviewed as well as a wide range of additional books and executive briefings that will help you put these ideas, and many more, to work.

To connect with the gurus and participate in the annual *Thinkers 50* guru ranking survey, go to

www.business-minds.com/goto/gurus

Spreading knowledge is a great way to improve performance and enhance business relationships. If you found this book useful, then so might your colleagues or customers. If you would like to explore corporate purchases or custom editions personalized with your brand or message, then just get in touch at

www.business-minds.com/corporatesales

Visit our website at [**www.business-minds.com**]